LITTLE CHOUX TEMPTATIONS

Jialin Tian, Ph.D.

Photographs and Design by Jialin Tian

Step-by-Step Photographs by Yabin Yu

Little Choux Temptations

Jialin Tian, Ph.D.

Copyright © 2017 by Jialin Tian

Photographs copyright © 2017 by Jialin Tian and Yabin Yu

All rights reserved. No part of this book may be reproduced or transmitted in any form or by any means, electronic or mechanical, including photocopying, recording, or by any information storage and retrieval system, without permission in writing from the publisher.

Disclaimer: While every precaution has been taken in the preparation of this book, the publisher and author assume no responsibility for errors or omissions, or for damage or loss resulting directly or indirectly from the use of the information contained herein.

Published in the United States by
Jayca
2936 Burrows Ln
Ellicott City, MD 21043

Photographs and styling: Jialin Tian
Step-by-step photographs and author's photographs: Yabin Yu
Book design: Jialin Tian
Production manager: Yabin Yu

www.macaronmagic.com

ISBN 978-0-9837764-8-2

First Edition, Reprint Edition 2019

INTRODUCTION
6

1. FRUIT
Apple & Fennel
10
Pomegranate & Grapefruit
14
Passionfruit Caramel
18
Pear
22
Coconut
27
Fruit Chou-Cake
29

2. NUTS
Almond, Fig, & Chocolate
36
Pecan "Pop Choux"
39
Macadamia & Apricot
42
Pistachio & Cherry
46
Hazelnut, Lemon, & Basil
50

Spices & Coffee
56
Lemongrass & Strawberry
60
Orange Blossom
64

3. HERBS & SPICES
Sichuan Peppercorn & Sesame
68
Rosemary & Mint
72
Spice Chou-Tart
76

4. VEGGIES
Avocado
82
Beets
85
Carrots
88
Zucchini Doughnuts
91
Red Pepper & Mango
94

5. CLASSIC
Cream Puffs
100
Caramel
103
Chocolate
106
Vanilla
110
Hazelnut & Raspberry
114

INTRODUCTION

Light, airy, crispy, and now in bite size! In this second book on choux pastries, we discover the possibilities of wonderfully delectable choux in petite form. While the first volume of *Choux Temptation* focused on the fundamental techniques of producing various choux pastries using the traditional pâte à choux (choux paste) ingredients, this book explores the endless variations on the choux paste itself as well as delicious flavoring options for the filling components. Non-traditional ingredients such as nut oils, fruit and vegetable purees, and herbs and spices are incorporated into the choux paste to create unique textures, flavors, and appearance.

This book is divided into five chapters. The first three chapters are dedicated to three groups of ingredients—fruit, nuts, and spices. Each recipe emphasizes a particular ingredient that is used in both the choux paste and the filling options. In addition, instructions for creating two centerpieces are introduced for the

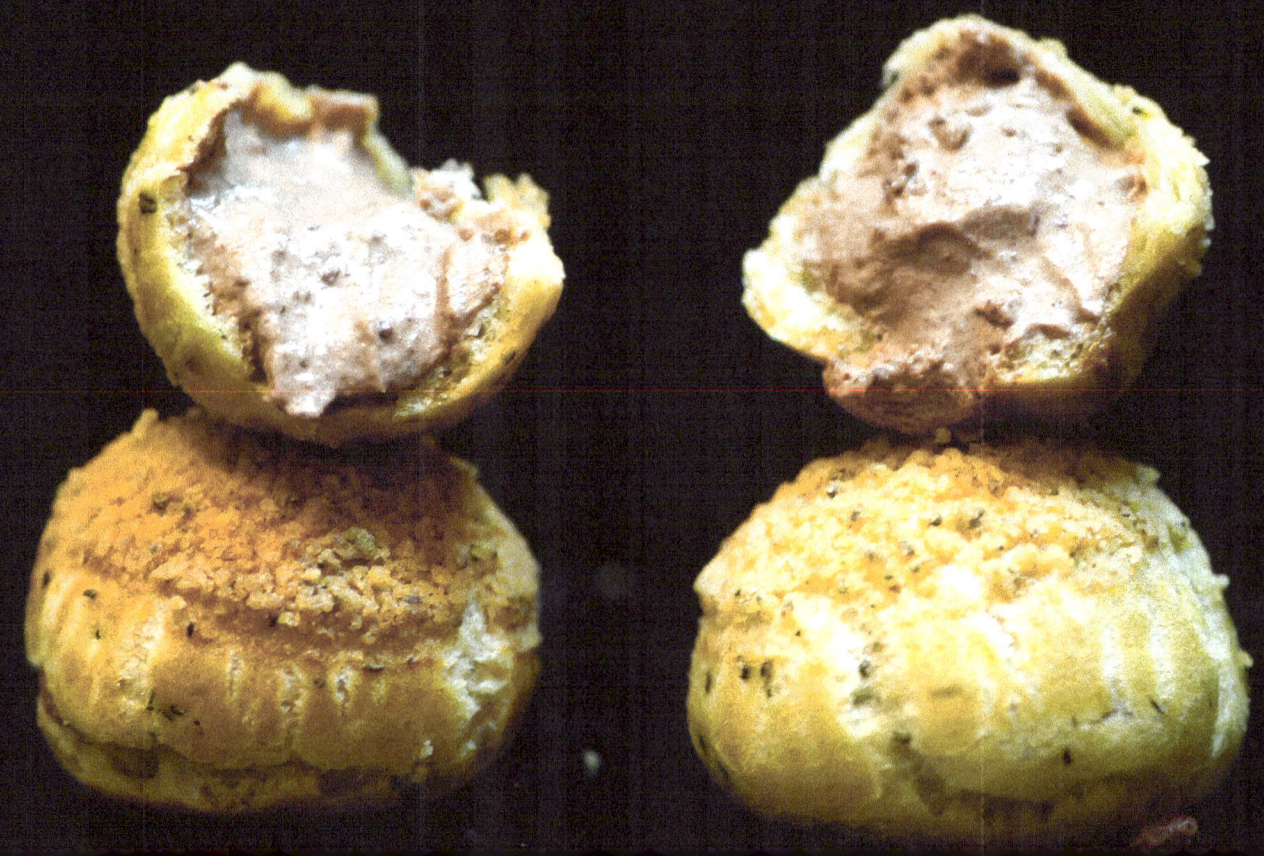

fruit and spice chapters. In chapter four, we present five innovative creations using vegetables such as beets, carrots, and zucchini. These "savory-turned-sweet" treats are delightful alternatives to the familiar pastry flavors. In the final chapter, we conclude our "adventure of choux" by revisiting some of the classic recipes for choux pastries.

Little Choux Temptations contains instructions for creating twenty-seven delectable and innovative petite choux pastries. Each recipe is accompanied by step-by-step photographs as well as photographs of the finished pastries. This book started as one of my afternoon brainstorming concepts, and it could not have become a reality without the help of my mother, Yabin. Once again, she was my action photographer, my sous-chef, my consultant, and so much more! I want to thank my father Richard for his help and support on our latest project. My deepest appreciation goes to Chefs Jacquy Pfeiffer and Sébastien Canonne at the French Pastry School in Chicago for their support and encouragement. Finally, thank you to pastry professionals and enthusiasts around the world for their feedback and support! Happy baking and have fun!

1. FRUIT

APPLE AND FENNEL

The familiar apple-caramel flavor is elevated with the addition of fennel, which adds another dimension of complexity to this wonderful dessert. You can use ready-made fondant; however, if you choose to make the fondant, be sure to make it at least a day in advance. The leftover fondant can be saved for other pastry applications.

Yield: about 50 3.8-cm/1.5-in mini choux

INGREDIENTS

Pastry Fondant (makes about 600 g/21.2 oz fondant):

500 g/17.6 oz granulated sugar

100 g/3.5 oz distilled water

100 g/3.5 oz glucose syrup

Apple Choux:

120 g/4.2 oz all-purpose flour

80 g/2.8 oz distilled water

100 g/3.5 oz green apple puree

2 g/0.071 oz (¼ tsp) kosher salt or fine sea salt

5 g/0.18 oz (1 tsp) granulated sugar

80 g/2.8 oz walnut oil

200 g/7.1 oz whole eggs (about 4 eggs)

1 whole egg for egg wash

Apple Caramel Cream:

100 g/3.5 oz green apple puree

100 g/3.5 oz granulated sugar

50 g/1.8 oz unsalted butter

Pastry Fondant (makes about 600 g/21.2 oz fondant):

1. Combine the sugar and water in a medium-sized stainless steel saucepan. Heat the mixture over medium heat. Stir constantly with a spatula until the sugar is dissolved.

2. When the sugar syrup comes to a boil, stir in the glucose syrup [1]. Bring the mixture back to a boil.

3. Insert a candy thermometer and stop stirring. Increase the heat to medium-high. Continue to cook the sugar; brush down the sides of the pan with a pastry brush dipped in cold water to prevent sugar crystals from forming.

4. Cook the sugar until it reaches 118°C/244°F. Let cool slightly. Pour the syrup into a food processor [2] and cover the food processor bowl tightly with plastic wrap.

5. Let the syrup cool to 80°C/176°F. Turn on the food processor. Mix until the syrup turns opaque, white, and glossy [3, 4].

6. Immediately transfer the white fondant into a plastic bag or other container. Cover and let it rest at room temperature overnight before using it. The fondant will become softer and more pliable.

Apple Choux:

1. Sift the flour onto a piece of parchment paper. Transfer the sifted flour to a bowl and reserve.

Pinch of salt

1 g/0.035 oz (½ tsp) ground toasted fennel seeds

100 g/3.5 oz mascarpone cheese, at room temperature

200 g/7.1 oz heavy whipping cream

Assembly and Decoration:

45 g/1.6 oz granulated sugar

35 g/1.2 oz distilled water

300 g/10.6 oz pastry fondant

Green gel food coloring

2. Combine the water, apple puree, salt, sugar, and walnut oil in a large stainless steel saucepan; heat the mixture over medium-high heat [5].

3. When the mixture comes to a boil, remove the saucepan from heat. Carefully whisk the sifted flour into the mixture [6]. When all the flour is incorporated into the liquid, shake off lumps of dough from the whisk and switch to a spatula or wooden spoon.

4. Return the saucepan to medium-low heat. Stir the paste using a folding motion to remove any remaining small lumps of flour [7]. Continue to cook for 2 to 3 minutes; stir constantly, using a folding motion to bring the dough pieces together, until a smooth and thick paste is obtained.

5. Transfer the dough to a mixer bowl. Attach the bowl to a mixer fitted with a paddle attachment. Mix the dough at medium speed for 10 to 15 seconds to release the steam.

6. Add the eggs one at a time while continuing to mix on medium speed [8]. Make sure each egg is incorporated before adding additional eggs. Scrape down the sides of the mixer bowl with a spatula if necessary. Increase the mixer speed to high. Mix for 10 to 20 seconds or until a smooth paste forms [9].

7. Meanwhile, line a half-sheet baking pan with a silicone baking mat or parchment paper. Preheat the oven to 191°C/375°F.

8. Fill a large pastry bag (45.7-cm/18-in) fitted with a 1.3-cm/0.5-in plain tip (#806) with the choux paste. Pipe the paste into 2.5-cm/1-in mounds with 2.5-cm/1-in spacing on the baking mat or parchment paper [10]. Brush the top with egg wash using a gentle dabbing motion [11].

9. Bake at 191°C/375°F for about 13 minutes until the choux are puffed up. Reduce the temperature to 177°C/350°F and bake for another 13 minutes until the choux are golden brown. Turn off the oven and leave the choux in the oven undisturbed for another 8 minutes. Remove the baked choux from the oven and let cool completely [12].

Apple Caramel Cream:

1. To make the apple caramel, place the green apple puree in a medium-sized stainless steel saucepan and set aside.

2. Place the sugar in a large stainless steel saucepan in an even layer. Dry melt the sugar over medium heat undisturbed for 3 to 5 minutes.

3. Meanwhile, heat the puree over high heat. Remove the pan from heat when the puree comes to a boil. Reserve.

4. When most of the sugar underneath the top layer of granules is melted and has turned a golden color, reduce the heat to low. Stir occasionally with a spatula to avoid burning the caramel.

5. When all of the sugar is melted and the caramel turns medium-dark amber [13] at around 180°C/356°F, pour the hot apple puree into the pan [14]. Stir vigorously to smooth out any lumps.

6. Continue to cook the caramel for another 2 to 3 minutes while stirring constantly. Cook until the caramel is smooth and velvety. Remove from heat, add butter, salt, and ground fennel seeds. Stir to combine [15].

7. Let the caramel cool slightly. Cover the surface of the caramel directly with plastic wrap. Allow the caramel to cool completely before using it.

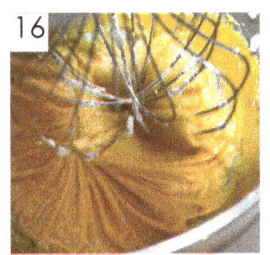

8. In a stand mixer fitted with a whisk attachment, whisk the mascarpone cheese and apple caramel until smooth [16].

9. In a stand mixer fitted with a whisk attachment, whisk the chilled heavy cream to medium peaks. Gently fold the whipped cream into the apple caramel-mascarpone cheese mixture until well combined [17]. Reserve the cream in the refrigerator until ready to use.

Assembly and Decoration:

1. Use a 1-cm/0.38-in fine star tip (#864) to punch a hole in the bottom of each chou [18].

2. Fill a large pastry bag (45.7-cm/18-in) fitted with a 0.8-cm/0.31-in plain tip (#803) with the apple caramel cream. Pipe the cream into each chou through the hole in the bottom [19].

3. To make the syrup for the fondant glaze, combine the sugar and water in a medium-sized saucepan. Bring the mixture to a boil and remove from heat. Let the syrup cool slightly.

4. Combine the syrup, pastry fondant, and green food coloring in a medium-sized mixing bowl. Gently heat the mixture over a double-boiler or in a microwave until the mixture reaches 37°C/98.6°F. Stir to combine. Do not heat the mixture hotter than 50°C/122°F.

5. Dip the filled chou into the green fondant glaze [20]. Gently shake off excess glaze and place the chou bottom-side down on a piece of parchment paper. Repeat until all the choux are glazed.

POMEGRANATE AND GRAPEFRUIT

Pomegranate-flavored choux filled with citrusy custard cream and covered in crunchy caramel, this is a festive dessert that is pleasing to the eye as well as the palate.

Yield: about 50 3.8-cm/1.5-in mini choux

INGREDIENTS

Pomegranate Choux:

120 g/4.2 oz all-purpose flour

100 g/3.5 oz distilled water

80 g/2.8 oz pomegranate juice

2 g/0.071 oz (¼ tsp) kosher salt or fine sea salt

5 g/0.18 oz (1 tsp) granulated sugar

80 g/2.8 oz unsalted butter

200 g/7.1 oz whole eggs (about 4 eggs)

1 whole egg for egg wash

Grapefruit Cream:

5 g/0.18 oz gelatin sheet (silver grade) or 4.2 g/0.15 oz powdered gelatin + 25.2 g/0.89 oz cold water

200 g/7.1 oz whole eggs

100 g/3.5 oz granulated sugar

150 g/5.3 oz grapefruit juice

15 g/0.53 oz grapefruit zest

200 g/7.1 oz unsalted butter, at room temperature

Pomegranate Choux:

1. Sift the flour onto a piece of parchment paper. Transfer the sifted flour to a bowl and reserve.

2. Combine the water, pomegranate juice, salt, sugar, and butter in a large stainless steel saucepan; heat the mixture over medium-high heat [1].

3. When the mixture comes to a boil, remove the saucepan from heat. Carefully whisk the sifted flour into the mixture [2]. When all the flour is incorporated into the liquid, shake off lumps of dough from the whisk and switch to a spatula or wooden spoon.

4. Return the saucepan to medium-low heat. Stir the paste using a folding motion to remove any remaining small lumps of flour [3]. Continue to cook for 2 to 3 minutes; stir constantly, using a folding motion to bring the dough pieces together, until a smooth and thick paste is obtained.

5. Transfer the dough to a mixer bowl. Attach the bowl to a mixer fitted with a paddle attachment. Mix the dough at medium speed for 10 to 15 seconds to release the steam.

6. Add the eggs one at a time while continuing to mix on medium speed [4]. Make sure each egg is incorporated before adding additional eggs. Scrape down the sides of the mixer bowl with a spatula if necessary. Increase the mixer speed to high. Mix for 10 to 20 seconds or until a smooth paste forms.

7. Meanwhile, line a half-sheet baking pan with a silicone baking mat or parchment paper. Preheat the oven to 191°C/375°F.

Assembly and Decoration:

500 g/17.6 oz granulated sugar

200 g/7.1 oz distilled water

100 g/3.5 oz glucose syrup

Red gel food coloring

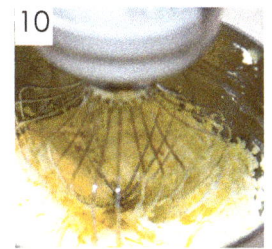
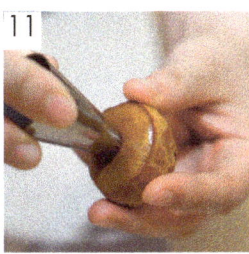

8. Fill a large pastry bag (45.7-cm/18-in) fitted with a 1.3-cm/0.5-in plain tip (#806) with the choux paste. Pipe the paste into 2.5-cm/1-in mounds with 2.5-cm/1-in spacing on the baking mat or parchment paper [5]. Brush the top with egg wash using a gentle dabbing motion [6].

9. Bake at 191°C/375°F for about 13 minutes until the choux are puffed up. Reduce the temperature to 177°C/350°F and bake for another 13 minutes until the choux are golden brown. Turn off the oven and leave the choux in the oven undisturbed for another 8 minutes. Remove the baked choux from the oven and let cool completely.

Grapefruit Cream:

1. In a medium-sized bowl, bloom the sheet gelatin in plenty of cold water. If powdered gelatin is used, sprinkle the powder over 25.2 g/0.89 oz cold water in the bowl. Let the gelatin bloom for at least 10 minutes before using.

2. Combine eggs, sugar, grapefruit juice, and zest in a medium-sized stainless steel saucepan. Heat the mixture over medium heat [7].

3. Gently whisk the mixture to allow even heating. Cook the mixture to 85°C/185°F and remove the pan from the heat. Take care not to over-heat the mixture; otherwise, the eggs in the mixture will coagulate. Let cool slightly.

4. Meanwhile, squeeze excess water out of the bloomed sheet gelatin and add the gelatin to the grapefruit mixture [8]. If powdered gelatin is used, add the entire contents to the grapefruit mixture. Stir to combine.

5. Pass the mixture through a fine mesh strainer [9]. Cover the surface of the grapefruit mixture with plastic wrap. Let cool completely.

6. Combine the grapefruit mixture and softened butter in a mixer bowl. Attach the bowl to a stand mixer fitted with a whisk attachment. Whisk until the cream is light and smooth [10]. Allow the cream to set in the refrigerator for 2 hours before using.

Assembly and Decoration:

1. Use a 1-cm/0.38-in fine star tip (#864) to punch a hole in the bottom of each chou [11].

2. To make the dipping caramel, combine the sugar and water in a medium-sized stainless steel saucepan. Heat the mixture over medium heat. Stir with a spatula constantly until the sugar is dissolved; skim off any impurities or foam that flow to the top.

3. When the sugar syrup comes to a boil, stir in the glucose syrup. Bring the mixture back to a boil.

4. Insert a candy thermometer and stop stirring. Increase the heat to medium-high. Continue to cook the sugar; brush down the sides of the pan with a pastry brush dipped in cold water to prevent sugar crystals from forming.

5. Cook the sugar until it reaches 160°C/320°F, about 15 to 20 minutes' cooking time. Remove from heat, and add a few drops of red food coloring. Stir to combine.

6. Allow the bubbles to subside slightly. Transfer the caramel to a heat-proof pitcher, and then pour a small amount of caramel into the cavities of 4.1-cm/1.6-in half-sphere silicone molds to about ⅓ way full [12].

7. Quickly insert the choux into caramel-filled molds with the bottom-side up [13]. Let the caramel harden completely before continuing.

Note: If silicone molds are not available, you can dip the choux directly into the caramel and place the glazed choux on a silicone baking mat or a piece of parchment paper with the caramel-coated side down.

8. Fill a large pastry bag (45.7-cm/18-in) fitted with a 0.8-cm/0.31-in plain tip (#803) with the grapefruit cream. Pipe the cream into each chou through the hole in the bottom [14].

9. Carefully remove the filled choux from the silicone molds [15, 16].

PASSIONFRUIT CARAMEL

This pastry has all the components that one can ask for in a dessert—airy and crispy choux, sweet and tropical passionfruit caramel, light and soft vanilla cream, topped with crunchy meringue dots and fresh raspberries. Although it takes a bit of effort to make, it is definitely worth it! You can make the meringue dots and passionfruit caramel a day in advance.

Yield: about 30 6.4-cm/2.5-in mini éclairs

INGREDIENTS

Meringue Dots:

100 g/3.5 oz egg white

180 g/6.3 oz granulated sugar

Red gel food coloring

Mini Éclairs:

120 g/4.2 oz all-purpose flour

180 g/6.3 oz distilled water

2 g/0.071 oz (¼ tsp) kosher salt or fine sea salt

5 g/0.18 oz (1 tsp) granulated sugar

80 g/2.8 oz grapeseed oil

200 g/7.1 oz whole eggs (about 4 eggs)

1 whole egg for egg wash

Passionfruit Caramel:

40 g/1.4 oz passionfruit puree

60 g/2.1 oz heavy whipping cream

1 vanilla bean

100 g/3.5 oz granulated sugar

Meringue Dots:

1. Combine egg whites and sugar in a mixer bowl. Place the bowl over a saucepan filled with simmering water over medium-low heat [1].

2. Beat the egg whites and sugar with a balloon whisk constantly until the mixture reaches 45°C/113°F.

3. Remove the mixer bowl from the water bath, and then attach the bowl to a stand mixer fitted with a whisk attachment. Add a few drops of red food coloring if desired. Beat the mixture on high speed until stiff, glossy peaks form and the meringue has cooled to room temperature [2].

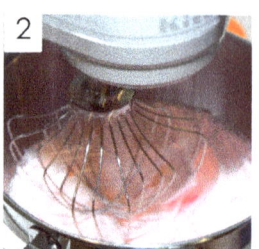

4. Preheat the oven to 104°C/220°F. Fill a large pastry bag (45.7-cm/18-in) fitted with a 1-cm/0.38-in plain tip (#804) with the meringue. Pipe the meringue into small dots on a baking pan lined with baking mat or parchment paper [3]. Bake for about 45 minutes [4]. Let cool completely before using.

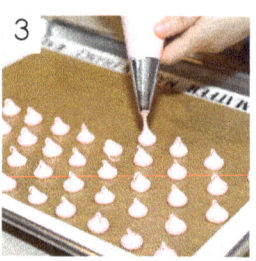

Mini Éclairs:

1. Sift the flour onto a piece of parchment paper. Transfer the sifted flour to a bowl and reserve.

2. Combine the water, salt, sugar, and grapeseed oil in a large stainless steel saucepan; heat the mixture over medium-high heat [5].

3. When the mixture comes to a boil, remove the saucepan from heat. Carefully whisk the sifted flour into the mixture [6, 7]. When all the flour is incorporated into the liquid, shake off lumps of dough from the whisk and switch to a spatula or wooden spoon.

70 g/2.5 oz unsalted butter, at room temperature

Pinch of salt

Vanilla Chantilly Cream:

130 g/4.6 oz mascarpone cheese

400 g/14.1 oz heavy whipping cream

60 g/2.1 oz granulated sugar

1 vanilla bean

Assembly and Decoration:

Fresh raspberries

4. Return the saucepan to medium-low heat. Stir the paste using a folding motion to remove any remaining small lumps of flour. Continue to cook for 2 to 3 minutes; stir constantly, using a folding motion to bring the dough pieces together, until a smooth and thick paste is obtained.

5. Transfer the dough to a mixer bowl. Attach the bowl to a mixer fitted with a paddle attachment. Mix the dough at medium speed for 10 to 15 seconds to release the steam.

6. Add the eggs one at a time while continuing to mix on medium speed [8]. Make sure each egg is incorporated before adding additional eggs. Scrape down the sides of the mixer bowl with a spatula if necessary. Increase the mixer speed to high. Mix for 10 to 20 seconds or until a smooth paste forms [9].

7. Meanwhile, line a half-sheet baking pan with a silicone baking mat or parchment paper.

8. Preheat the oven to 191°C/375°F. Fill a large pastry bag (45.7-cm/18-in) fitted with a 1.1-cm/0.44-in fine star tip (#865) with the choux paste. Pipe the paste into 6.4-cm/2.5-in logs with 2.5-cm/1-in spacing on the baking mat or parchment paper [10]. Brush the top with egg wash using a gentle dabbing motion [11].

9. Bake at 191°C/375°F for about 15 minutes until the éclairs are puffed up. Reduce the temperature to 177°C/350°F and bake for another 15 minutes until the éclairs are golden brown. Turn off the oven and leave the éclairs in the oven undisturbed for another 10 minutes. Remove the baked éclairs from the oven and let cool completely [12].

Passionfruit Caramel:

1. Place the passionfruit puree and heavy cream in a medium-sized stainless steel saucepan. Use a paring knife to split the vanilla bean lengthwise. Scrape off the vanilla seeds using the back of the knife. Add the vanilla seeds to the mixture.

2. Place the sugar in a large stainless steel saucepan in an even layer. Dry melt the sugar over medium heat undisturbed for 3 to 5 minutes.

3. Meanwhile, heat the passionfruit and cream mixture over high heat. Remove the pan from heat when the mixture comes to a boil. Reserve.

4. When most of the sugar underneath the top layer of granules is melted and has turned a golden color, reduce the heat to low. Stir occasionally with a spatula to avoid burning the caramel [13].

5. When all of the sugar is melted and the caramel turns medium-dark amber, at around 180°C/356°F, stir in the softened butter [14], and then pour the hot passionfruit mixture into the pan [15]. Stir vigorously to smooth out any lumps.

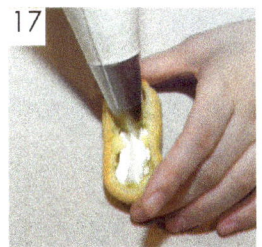
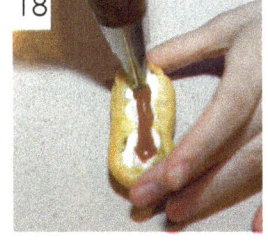

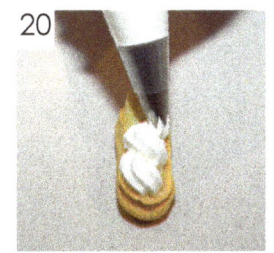

6. Continue to cook the caramel for another minute while stirring constantly. Cook until the caramel is smooth and velvety. Remove from heat, add salt, and stir to combine.

7. Let the caramel cool slightly. Cover the surface of the caramel directly with plastic wrap. Allow the caramel to cool completely. Chill the caramel in the refrigerator for a few hours.

Vanilla Chantilly Cream:

1. In a mixer bowl, combine the mascarpone cheese, heavy cream, and sugar. Use a paring knife to split the vanilla bean lengthwise. Scrape off the vanilla seeds using the back of the knife. Add the vanilla seeds to the mixture.

2. Attach the mixer bowl to a mixer fitted with a whisk attachment. Whisk the mixture on medium speed until the mixture thickens slightly. Increase the speed to high and whisk the mixture until stiff peaks form [16]. Do not over-beat.

Assembly and Decoration:

1. Using a serrated knife, cut off the top ⅓ of each éclair and reserve the top.

2. Fill a large pastry bag (45.7-cm/18-in) fitted with a 1-cm/0.38-in star tip (#824) with the Chantilly cream. Pipe the cream into the bottom portion of each éclair [17].

3. Fill another large pastry bag (45.7-cm/18-in) fitted with a 0.64-cm/0.25-in plain tip (#802) with the passionfruit caramel. Pipe the caramel on top of the cream [18].

4. Place the reserved éclair top, glossy side down, on top of the caramel [19]. Pipe more Chantilly cream [20]. Arrange the meringue dots and fresh raspberries on top of the cream [21].

FRUIT

PEAR

In this autumn-inspired dessert, pear-flavored choux are filled with pear-mascarpone cream accented with just a hint of spice. The cassia flower jam adds an interesting note to the filling, but if it is difficult to find, you can omit this component.

Yield: about 50 3.8-cm/1.5-in mini choux

INGREDIENTS

Pear Choux:

120 g/4.2 oz all-purpose flour

80 g/2.8 oz distilled water

100 g/3.5 oz pear puree

2 g/0.071 oz (¼ tsp) kosher salt or fine sea salt

5 g/0.18 oz (1 tsp) granulated sugar

80 g/2.8 oz unsalted butter

200 g/7.1 oz whole eggs (about 4 eggs)

1 whole egg for egg wash

Pear Cream:

5 g/0.18 oz gelatin sheet (silver grade) or 4.2 g/0.15 oz powdered gelatin + 25.2 g/0.89 oz cold water

210 g/7.4 oz pear puree

2 star anise pods

20 g/0.71 oz (1 Tbsp) cassia flower jam

30 g/1.1 oz granulated sugar

150 g/5.3 oz mascarpone cheese, at room temperature

Pear Choux:

1. Sift the flour onto a piece of parchment paper. Transfer the sifted flour to a bowl and reserve.

2. Combine the water, pear puree, salt, sugar, and butter in a large stainless steel saucepan; heat the mixture over medium-high heat [1].

3. When the mixture comes to a boil, remove the saucepan from heat. Carefully whisk the sifted flour into the mixture [2]. When all the flour is incorporated into the liquid, shake off lumps of dough from the whisk and switch to a spatula or wooden spoon.

4. Return the saucepan to medium-low heat. Stir the paste using a folding motion to remove any remaining small lumps of flour [3]. Continue to cook for 2 to 3 minutes; stir constantly, using a folding motion to bring the dough pieces together, until a smooth and thick paste is obtained.

5. Transfer the dough to a mixer bowl. Attach the bowl to a mixer fitted with a paddle attachment. Mix the dough at medium speed for 10 to 15 seconds to release the steam.

6. Add the eggs one at a time while continuing to mix on medium speed [4]. Make sure each egg is incorporated before adding additional eggs. Scrape down the sides of the mixer bowl with a spatula if necessary. Increase the mixer speed to high. Mix for 10 to 20 seconds or until a smooth paste forms.

7. Meanwhile, line a half-sheet baking pan with a silicone baking mat or parchment paper. Preheat the oven to 191°C/375°F.

250 g/8.8 oz heavy whipping cream

Assembly and Decoration:

500 g/17.6 oz granulated sugar

200 g/7.1 oz distilled water

100 g/3.5 oz glucose syrup

Yellow gel food coloring

8. Fill a large pastry bag (45.7-cm/18-in) fitted with a 1.3-cm/0.5-in plain tip (#806) with the choux paste. Pipe the paste into 2.5-cm/1-in mounds with 2.5-cm/1-in spacing on the baking mat or parchment paper [5]. Brush the top with egg wash using a gentle dabbing motion.

9. Bake at 191°C/375°F for about 13 minutes until the choux are puffed up. Reduce the temperature to 177°C/350°F and bake for another 13 minutes until the choux are golden brown. Turn off the oven and leave the choux in the oven undisturbed for another 8 minutes. Remove the baked choux from the oven and let cool completely [6].

Pear Cream:

1. In a medium-sized bowl, bloom the sheet gelatin in plenty of cold water. If powdered gelatin is used, sprinkle the powder over 25.2 g/0.89 oz cold water in the bowl. Let the gelatin bloom for at least 10 minutes before using.

2. In a medium-sized stainless steel saucepan, combine the pear puree, star anise pods, cassia flower jam, and sugar [7].

3. Bring the mixture to a boil, and remove from heat. Cover the saucepan and allow the mixture to infuse for about 10 minutes.

4. Meanwhile, squeeze excess water out of the bloomed sheet gelatin. Melt the bloomed sheet gelatin or powdered gelatin in a microwave for a few seconds. Do not overheat.

5. Remove the star anise pods from the saucepan. Add the melted gelatin into the pear mixture, and stir to combine. Cover the surface of the pear jelly with plastic wrap. Let cool completely.

6. In a stand mixer fitted with a whisk attachment, whisk the mascarpone cheese until smooth. Gradually add the pear jelly and whisk until the mixture is smooth and homogenous.

7. Whisk the chilled heavy cream to stiff peaks using a mixer or by hand [8]. Gently fold the whipped cream into the pear-mascarpone cheese mixture until well combined [9]. Reserve the cream in the refrigerator until ready to use.

Assembly and Decoration:

1. Use a 1-cm/0.38-in fine star tip (#864) to punch a hole in the bottom of each chou [10].

2. To make the dipping caramel, combine the sugar and water in a medium-sized stainless steel saucepan. Heat the mixture over medium heat. Stir with a spatula constantly until the sugar is dissolved; skim off any impurities or foam that flow to the top.

3. When the sugar syrup comes to a boil, stir in the glucose syrup. Bring the mixture back to a boil [11].

4. Insert a candy thermometer and stop stirring [12]. Increase the heat to medium-high. Continue to cook the sugar; brush down the sides of the pan with a pastry brush dipped in cold water to prevent sugar crystals from forming [13].

5. Cook the sugar until it reaches 160°C/320°F, about 15 to 20 minutes' cooking time. Remove from heat, and add a few drops of yellow food coloring. Stir to combine.

6. Allow the bubbles to subside slightly. Transfer the caramel to a heat-proof pitcher, and then pour a small amount of caramel into the cavities of 4.1-cm/1.6-in half-sphere silicone molds to about ⅓ way full [14].

7. Quickly insert the choux into caramel-filled molds with the bottom-side up [15]. Let the caramel harden completely before continuing.

Note: If silicone molds are not available, you can dip the choux directly into the caramel and place the glazed choux on a silicone baking mat or a piece of parchment paper with the caramel-coated side down.

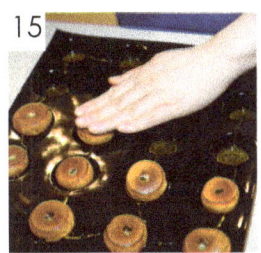
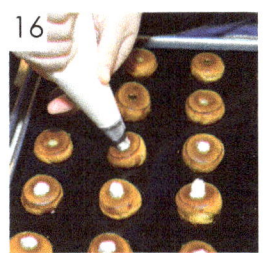

8. Fill a large pastry bag (45.7-cm/18-in) fitted with a 0.8-cm/0.31-in plain tip (#803) with the pear cream. Pipe the cream into each chou through the hole in the bottom [16].

9. Carefully remove the filled choux from the silicone molds [17, 18].

FRUIT 25

COCONUT

I started experimenting with alternative choux paste ingredients with this recipe. The coconut puree and oil in the choux paste produce distinctive flavors and texture when compared to the original water, milk, and butter combination. The coconut custard cream accented with dark rum intensifies the coconut aroma of this tropical-flavored dessert.

Yield: about 50 3.8-cm/1.5-in mini choux

INGREDIENTS

Coconut Choux:

120 g/4.2 oz all-purpose flour

80 g/2.8 oz distilled water

100 g/3.5 oz coconut puree

2 g/0.071 oz (¼ tsp) kosher salt or fine sea salt

5 g/0.18 oz (1 tsp) granulated sugar

80 g/2.8 oz coconut oil

200 g/7.1 oz whole eggs (about 4 eggs)

1 whole egg for egg wash

Unsweetened shredded coconut

Coconut Cream:

100 g/3.5 oz egg yolks

60 g/2.1 oz granulated sugar

40 g/1.4 oz cornstarch

400 g/14.1 oz coconut puree

40 g/1.4 oz unsalted butter, at room temperature

15 g/0. 53 oz (1 Tbsp) dark rum

200 g/7.1 oz heavy whipping cream

Coconut Choux:

1. Sift the flour onto a piece of parchment paper. Transfer the sifted flour to a bowl and reserve.

2. Combine the water, coconut puree, salt, sugar, and coconut oil in a large stainless steel saucepan; heat the mixture over medium-high heat [1].

3. When the mixture comes to a boil, remove the saucepan from heat. Carefully whisk the sifted flour into the mixture [2]. When all the flour is incorporated into the liquid, shake off lumps of dough from the whisk and switch to a spatula or wooden spoon.

4. Return the saucepan to medium-low heat. Stir the paste using a folding motion to remove any remaining small lumps of flour. Continue to cook for 2 to 3 minutes; stir constantly, using a folding motion to bring the dough pieces together, until a smooth and thick paste is obtained [3].

5. Transfer the dough to a mixer bowl. Attach the bowl to a mixer fitted with a paddle attachment. Mix the dough at medium speed for 10 to 15 seconds to release the steam.

6. Add the eggs one at a time while continuing to mix on medium speed. Make sure each egg is incorporated before adding additional eggs. Scrape down the sides of the mixer bowl with a spatula if necessary. Increase the mixer speed to high. Mix for 10 to 20 seconds or until a smooth paste forms [4].

7. Meanwhile, line a half-sheet baking pan with a silicone baking mat or parchment paper. Preheat the oven to 191°C/375°F.

8. Fill a large pastry bag (45.7-cm/18-in) fitted with a 1.3-cm/0.5-in plain tip (#806) with the choux paste. Pipe the paste into 2.5-cm/1-in mounds with 2.5-cm/1-in spacing on the baking mat or parchment paper [5]. Brush the top with egg wash using a gentle dabbing motion [6]. Sprinkle the choux with shredded coconut [7].

9. Bake at 191°C/375°F for about 13 minutes until the choux are puffed up. Reduce the temperature to 177°C/350°F and bake for another 13 minutes until the choux are golden brown. Turn off the oven and leave the choux in the oven undisturbed for another 8 minutes. Remove the baked choux from the oven and let cool completely [8].

Coconut Cream:

1. Combine egg yolks, sugar, and cornstarch in a stainless steel mixing bowl. Mix well with a balloon whisk [9]. Set aside.

2. Heat the coconut puree mixture over medium-high heat. Remove from heat when it comes to a boil. Pour about half of the hot liquid into the reserved egg yolk mixture while whisking vigorously [10]. Pour the mixture back into the pan. Cook the mixture over medium-low heat while whisking constantly for 1 to 2 minutes until the mixture thickens [11]. Let cool slightly. Stir in the softened butter and rum. Mix well.

3. Cover the surface of the coconut pastry cream with plastic wrap. Let cool to room temperature.

4. Place the coconut pastry cream in a mixer bowl. Beat with a stand mixer fitted with a wire whisk attachment on medium-high speed until the cream is smooth.

5. Whip the chilled heavy cream to stiff peaks by hand or using a mixer. Fold about ⅓ of the whipped cream into the coconut pastry cream using a spatula. Mix until the mixture is homogenous. Gently fold in the remaining ⅔ of the whipped cream [12]. Reserve.

Assembly and Decoration:

1. Use a 1-cm/0.38-in fine star tip (#864) to punch a hole in the bottom of each chou [13].

2. Fill a large pastry bag (45.7-cm/18-in) fitted with a 0.8-cm/0.31-in plain tip (#803) with the coconut cream. Pipe the cream into each chou through the hole in the bottom [14].

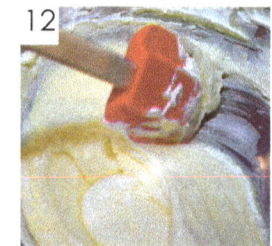

LITTLE CHOUX TEMPTATIONS

FRUIT CHOU-CAKE

No doubt this is a gorgeous centerpiece to showcase your fruit-inspired choux creations. This colorful and delicious pastry is the perfect dessert for any summer gathering. You can select any little choux when assembling this cake. This is the time to impress everyone with your imagination and creativity!

Yield: one 20-cm/8-in cake

INGREDIENTS

Chou-Cake Base:

120 g/4.2 oz all-purpose flour

100 g/3.5 oz distilled water

100 g/3.5 oz whole milk

2 g/0.071 oz (¼ tsp) kosher salt or fine sea salt

5 g/0.18 oz (1 tsp) granulated sugar

80 g/2.8 oz unsalted butter

200 g/7.1 oz whole eggs (about 4 eggs)

1 whole egg for egg wash

Vanilla Mousseline Cream:

80 g/2.8 oz egg yolks

50 g/1.8 oz granulated sugar (A)

30 g/1.1 oz cornstarch

400 g/14.1 oz whole milk

50 g/1.8 oz granulated sugar (B)

1 vanilla bean

220 g/7.8 oz unsalted butter, at room temperature

Chou-Cake Base:

1. Sift the flour onto a piece of parchment paper. Transfer the sifted flour to a bowl and reserve.

2. Combine the water, milk, salt, sugar, and butter in a large stainless steel saucepan; heat the mixture over medium-high heat [1].

3. When the mixture comes to a boil, remove the saucepan from heat. Carefully whisk the sifted flour into the mixture [2]. When all the flour is incorporated into the liquid, shake off lumps of dough from the whisk and switch to a spatula or wooden spoon.

4. Return the saucepan to medium-low heat. Stir the paste using a folding motion to remove any remaining small lumps of flour. Continue to cook for 2 to 3 minutes; stir constantly, using a folding motion to bring the dough pieces together, until a smooth and thick paste is obtained [3].

5. Transfer the dough to a mixer bowl. Attach the bowl to a mixer fitted with a paddle attachment. Mix the dough at medium speed for 10 to 15 seconds to release the steam.

6. Add the eggs one at a time while continuing to mix on medium speed. Make sure each egg is incorporated before adding additional eggs. Scrape down the sides of the mixer bowl with a spatula if necessary. Increase the mixer speed to high. Mix for 10 to 20 seconds or until a smooth paste forms [4].

7. Meanwhile, line a half-sheet baking pan with a silicone baking mat or parchment paper. Butter the inner rim of a 20-cm/8-in cake ring (6-cm/2.4-in in height). Place the cake ring on the baking mat.

Assembly and Decoration:

8 to 10 assorted fruit mini choux

Fresh assorted berries (strawberries, blueberries, and raspberries)

Fresh mint leaves

Powdered sugar

8. Preheat the oven to 191°C/375°F. Fill a large pastry bag (45.7-cm/18-in) fitted with a 1.7-cm/0.67-in fine star tip (#869) with the choux paste. Pipe a ring of choux paste along the inner edge of the cake ring on the baking mat or parchment paper. Pipe a second circle inside the first ring of paste [5]. Finally, pipe a third circle on top of the first two rings [6]. Brush the top with egg wash using a gentle dabbing motion [7].

9. Bake at 191°C/375°F for about 35 minutes until the chou-cake is puffed up. Reduce the temperature to 177°C/350°F and bake for another 25 minutes until the chou-cake is golden brown. Turn off the oven and leave the chou-cake in the oven undisturbed for another 10 minutes. Remove the baked chou-cake from the oven and let cool completely.

Vanilla Mousseline Cream:

1. Combine egg yolks, sugar (A), and cornstarch in a stainless steel mixing bowl. Mix well with a balloon whisk [8]. Set aside.

2. Place the milk and sugar (B) in a medium-sized stainless steel saucepan. Use a paring knife to split the vanilla bean lengthwise. Scrape off the vanilla seeds using the back of the knife. Add the vanilla bean halves and seeds to the saucepan.

3. Heat the milk mixture over medium-high heat. Remove from heat when it comes to a boil. Pour about half of the hot liquid into the reserved egg yolk mixture while whisking vigorously [9]. Pour the mixture back into the pan. Remove the vanilla bean halves. Cook the mixture over medium-low heat while whisking constantly for 1 to 2 minutes until the mixture thickens [10].

4. Cover the surface of the pastry cream with plastic wrap. Let cool to room temperature.

5. Place the pastry cream in a mixer bowl. Beat with a stand mixer fitted with a wire whisk attachment on medium-high speed until the cream is smooth.

6. Reduce the mixer speed to medium-low and whisk in the softened butter in small increments. Make sure each addition of butter is thoroughly incorporated before adding more. Scrape down the sides of the bowl with a spatula if necessary.

7. Once all the butter is incorporated, adjust the mixer speed to medium-high. Continue to beat for a few more minutes until the cream is light and fluffy [11]. Reserve.

Assembly and Decoration:

1. Using a serrated knife, cut off the top ⅓ of chou-cake [12]. Trim off the uneven edges from the top portion [13].

2. Fill a large pastry bag (45.7-cm/18-in) fitted with a 1-cm/0.38-in fine star tip (#864) with the vanilla mousseline cream. Pipe some cream into the bottom portion of the chou-cake [14].

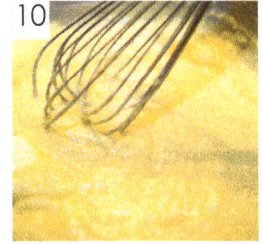

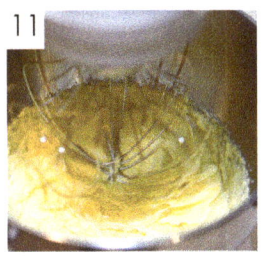 

3. With the glossy and smooth side facing down, place the top portion of the chou-cake on top of the cream. Pipe more cream on top [15].

4. Place the assorted fruit mini choux on the cream [16]. Pipe more cream around the min choux [17]. Arrange the fresh berries and mint leaves around the choux [18]. Dust the cake with powdered sugar if desired.

2. NUTS

Almond, Fig, & Chocolate
Pecan "Pop Choux"
Macadamia & Apricot
Pistachio & Cherry
Hazelnut, Lemon, & Basil

ALMOND, FIG, AND CHOCOLATE

In this recipe, the traditional ingredients of milk and butter are replaced with almond milk and roasted almond oil. The resulting choux have a much lighter and crunchier texture with a hint of sweet almond. For the filling, the fig, mascarpone cheese, and dark chocolate make the perfect trio.

Yield: about 30 6.4-cm/2.5-in mini éclairs

INGREDIENTS

Almond Mini Éclairs:

120 g/4.2 oz all-purpose flour

180 g/6.3 oz almond milk, unsweetened and unflavored

2 g/0.071 oz (¼ tsp) kosher salt or fine sea salt

5 g/0.18 oz (1 tsp) granulated sugar

80 g/2.8 oz roasted almond oil

200 g/7.1 oz whole eggs (about 4 eggs)

1 whole egg for egg wash

Slivered almonds

Fig Cream:

5 g/0.18 oz gelatin sheet (silver grade) or 4.2 g/0.15 oz powdered gelatin + 25.2 g/0.89 oz cold water

240 g/8.5 oz fig puree

50 g/1.8 oz granulated sugar

150 g/5.3 oz mascarpone cheese, at room temperature

250 g/8.8 oz heavy whipping cream

Assembly and Decoration:

60 g/2.1 oz bittersweet chocolate couverture, chopped

Powdered sugar

Almond Mini Éclairs:

1. Sift the flour onto a piece of parchment paper. Transfer the sifted flour to a bowl and reserve.

2. Combine the almond milk, salt, sugar, and almond oil in a large stainless steel saucepan; heat the mixture over medium-high heat.

3. When the mixture comes to a boil, remove the saucepan from heat. Carefully whisk the sifted flour into the mixture [1, 2]. When all the flour is incorporated into the liquid, shake off lumps of dough from the whisk and switch to a spatula or wooden spoon.

4. Return the saucepan to medium-low heat. Stir the paste using a folding motion to remove any remaining small lumps of flour [3]. Continue to cook for 2 to 3 minutes; stir constantly, using a folding motion to bring the dough pieces together, until a smooth and thick paste is obtained.

5. Transfer the dough to a mixer bowl. Attach the bowl to a mixer fitted with a paddle attachment. Mix the dough at medium speed for 10 to 15 seconds to release the steam.

6. Add the eggs one at a time while continuing to mix on medium speed [4]. Make sure each egg is incorporated before adding additional eggs. Scrape down the sides of the mixer bowl with a spatula if necessary. Increase the mixer speed to high. Mix for 10 to 20 seconds or until a smooth paste forms.

7. Meanwhile, line a half-sheet baking pan with a silicone baking mat or parchment paper.

8. Preheat the oven to 191°C/375°F. Fill a large pastry bag (45.7-cm/18-in) fitted with a 1.1-cm/0.44-in fine star tip (#865) with the choux paste. Pipe the paste

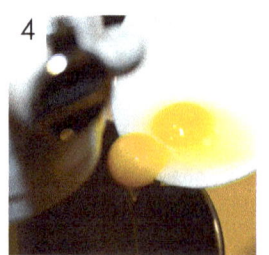

into 6.4-cm/2.5-in logs with 2.5-cm/1-in spacing on the baking mat or parchment paper [5]. Brush the top with egg wash using a gentle dabbing motion. Sprinkle slivered almonds on top [6].

9. Bake at 191°C/375°F for about 15 minutes until the éclairs are puffed up. Reduce the temperature to 177°C/350°F and bake for another 15 minutes until the éclairs are golden brown. Turn off the oven and leave the éclairs in the oven undisturbed for another 10 minutes. Remove the baked éclairs from the oven and let cool completely [7].

Fig Cream:

1. In a medium-sized bowl, bloom the sheet gelatin in plenty of cold water. If powdered gelatin is used, sprinkle the powder over 25.2 g/0.89 oz cold water in the bowl. Let the gelatin bloom for at least 10 minutes before using.

2. Combine the fig puree and sugar in a medium-sized stainless steel saucepan. Mix well with a balloon whisk [8]. Bring the mixture to 71°C/160°F over medium-high heat. Let cool slightly.

3. Meanwhile, squeeze excess water out of the bloomed sheet gelatin and add the gelatin to the fig mixture. If powdered gelatin is used, add the entire contents to the fig mixture. Stir to combine. Cover the surface of the fig jelly with plastic wrap. Let cool completely.

4. In a stand mixer fitted with a whisk attachment, whisk the mascarpone cheese until smooth. Gradually add the fig jelly and whisk until the mixture is smooth and homogenous [9].

5. Whisk the chilled heavy cream to stiff peaks using a mixer or by hand. Gently fold the whipped cream into the fig-mascarpone cheese mixture until well combined [10]. Reserve the cream in the refrigerator until ready to use.

Assembly and Decoration:

1. Using a serrated knife, cut off the top ⅓ of each éclair and reserve the cap [11].

2. Fill a large pastry bag (45.7-cm/18-in) fitted with a 1-cm/0.38-in star tip (#824) with the fig cream. Pipe the cream into the bottom portion of each éclair [12].

3. Sprinkle chopped chocolate pieces on top [13]. Placed the reserved cap on top of the cream. Dust the top with powdered sugar if desired [14].

PECAN "POP CHOUX"

A playful interpretation of popcorn, these amusing little bites will catch everyone's attention. Crunchy, nutty pecan chou-bites are baked with a pecan crumble topping and then coated with cinnamon sugar. They should be served while freshly baked, but I don't think they can last very long once you have tasted them.

Yield: about 160 mini pop choux

INGREDIENTS

Pecan Crumble Topping:

50 g/1.8 oz raw pecan nuts

50 g/1.8 oz all-purpose flour

50 g/1.8 oz light brown sugar

Pinch of salt

50 g/1.8 oz unsalted butter cubes, chilled

Pecan Choux:

120 g/4.2 oz all-purpose flour

180 g/6.3 oz distilled water

2 g/0.071 oz (¼ tsp) kosher salt or fine sea salt

5 g/0.18 oz (1 tsp) granulated sugar

80 g/2.8 oz roasted pecan oil

200 g/7.1 oz whole eggs (about 4 eggs)

1 whole egg for egg wash

Assembly and Decoration:

60 g/2.1 oz powdered sugar

5 g/0.18 oz (1 tsp) cinnamon powder

Pecan Crumble Topping:

1. Process the raw pecan nuts in a food processor for a few seconds. Add the flour, light brown sugar, and salt.

2. Pulse the food processor a few times to evenly distribute the ingredients.

3. Add the chilled butter pieces [1]. Pulse the machine a few more times until a crumbly consistency is obtained [2]. Do not over-mix.

4. Place the dough pieces on a baking tray. Break the larger pieces into pea-sized pieces [3]. Chill the crumbles in the refrigerator.

Pecan Choux:

1. Sift the flour onto a piece of parchment paper. Transfer the sifted flour to a bowl and reserve.

2. Combine the water, salt, sugar, and pecan oil in a large stainless steel saucepan [4]; heat the mixture over medium-high heat.

3. When the mixture comes to a boil, remove the saucepan from heat. Carefully whisk the sifted flour into the mixture. When all the flour is incorporated into the liquid, shake off lumps of dough from the whisk and switch to a spatula or wooden spoon.

4. Return the saucepan to medium-low heat. Stir the paste using a folding motion to remove any remaining small lumps of flour. Continue to cook for 2 to 3 minutes; stir constantly, using a folding motion to bring the dough pieces together, until a smooth and thick paste is obtained [5].

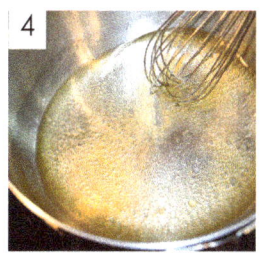

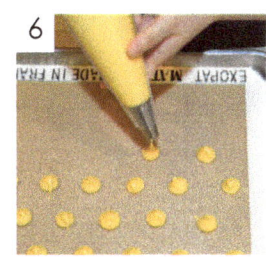

5. Transfer the dough to a mixer bowl. Attach the bowl to a mixer fitted with a paddle attachment. Mix the dough at medium speed for 10 to 15 seconds to release the steam.

6. Add the eggs one at a time while continuing to mix on medium speed. Make sure each egg is incorporated before adding additional eggs. Scrape down the sides of the mixer bowl with a spatula if necessary. Increase the mixer speed to high. Mix for 10 to 20 seconds or until a smooth paste forms.

7. Meanwhile, line a half-sheet baking pan with a silicone baking mat or parchment paper. Preheat the oven to 191°C/375°F.

8. Fill a large pastry bag (45.7-cm/18-in) fitted with a 1.3-cm/0.5-in plain tip (#806) with the choux paste. Pipe the paste into 1.3-cm/0.5-in mounds on the baking mat or parchment paper [6]. Brush the top with egg wash using a gentle dabbing motion [7]. Sprinkle the reserved pecan crumbles on top [8].

9. Bake at 191°C/375°F for about 12 minutes until the choux are puffed up. Reduce the temperature to 177°C/350°F and bake for another 12 minutes until the choux are golden brown. Turn off the oven and leave the choux in the oven undisturbed for another 6 minutes. Remove the baked choux from the oven and let cool completely [9].

Assembly and Decoration:

1. Mix the powdered sugar and cinnamon powder in a mixing bowl.

2. Toss the baked pecan pop choux in the cinnamon-sugar mixture [10]. Use a mesh strainer to remove excess cinnamon-sugar [11].

MACADAMIA AND APRICOT

In this nutty transformation, the classic choux paste is reinvented with macadamia nuts. The rich and slightly sweet macadamia nut is complemented with the tangy and fragrant apricot cream. Familiar yet exotic, this is an absolutely delightful dessert.

Yield: about 32 5-cm/2-in choux

INGREDIENTS

Macadamia Crumble Cookie Topping:

50 g/1.8 oz raw macadamia nuts

50 g/1.8 oz all-purpose flour

50 g/1.8 oz light brown sugar

Pinch of salt

50 g/1.8 oz unsalted butter cubes, at room temperature

15 g/0.53 oz white pearl sugar crystals (optional)

Macadamia Choux:

120 g/4.2 oz all-purpose flour

180 g/6.3 oz distilled water

2 g/0.071 oz (¼ tsp) kosher salt or fine sea salt

5 g/0.18 oz (1 tsp) granulated sugar

80 g/2.8 oz macadamia oil

200 g/7.1 oz whole eggs (about 4 eggs)

1 whole egg for egg wash

Macadamia Crumble Cookie Topping:

1. Process the raw macadamia nuts in a food processor for a few seconds. Add the flour, light brown sugar, and salt.

2. Pulse the food processor a few times to evenly distribute the ingredients.

3. Add the softened butter pieces [1]. Pulse the machine a few more times until a smooth dough forms [2]. Do not over-mix. Fold the pearl sugar crystals into the dough if desired.

4. Place the dough between two pieces of plastic wrap and flatten the dough slightly. Chill for 2 hours in the refrigerator.

5. Roll out the dough between two pieces of parchment paper to 2-mm/0.08-in thick [3]. Chill the dough in the refrigerator for about 45 minutes or in the freezer for about 10 minutes.

6. Remove the chilled dough from the refrigerator or freezer. Use a 2.8-cm/1.1-in round pastry cutter to cut out circular disks from the dough [4]. Return the cookie disks to the refrigerator or freezer until ready to use.

Macadamia Choux:

1. Sift the flour onto a piece of parchment paper. Transfer the sifted flour to a bowl and reserve.

2. Combine the water, salt, sugar, and macadamia oil in a large stainless steel saucepan; heat the mixture over medium-high heat [5].

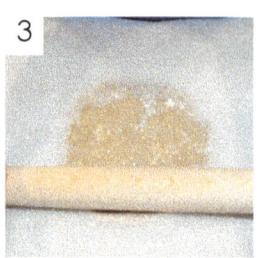

Apricot Cream:

5 g/0.18 oz gelatin sheet (silver grade) or 4.2 g/0.15 oz powdered gelatin + 25.2 g/0.89 oz cold water

240 g/8.5 oz apricot puree

50 g/1.8 oz granulated sugar

150 g/5.3 oz mascarpone cheese, at room temperature

200 g/7.1 oz heavy whipping cream

3. When the mixture comes to a boil, remove the saucepan from heat. Carefully whisk the sifted flour into the mixture [6, 7]. When all the flour is incorporated into the liquid, shake off lumps of dough from the whisk and switch to a spatula or wooden spoon.

4. Return the saucepan to medium-low heat. Stir the paste using a folding motion to remove any remaining small lumps of flour. Continue to cook for 2 to 3 minutes; stir constantly, using a folding motion to bring the dough pieces together, until a smooth and thick paste is obtained.

5. Transfer the dough to a mixer bowl. Attach the bowl to a mixer fitted with a paddle attachment. Mix the dough at medium speed for 10 to 15 seconds to release the steam.

6. Add the eggs one at a time while continuing to mix on medium speed [8]. Make sure each egg is incorporated before adding additional eggs. Scrape down the sides of the mixer bowl with a spatula if necessary. Increase the mixer speed to high. Mix for 10 to 20 seconds or until a smooth paste forms.

7. Meanwhile, line a half-sheet baking pan with a silicone baking mat or parchment paper. Preheat the oven to 191°C/375°F.

8. Fill a large pastry bag (45.7-cm/18-in) fitted with a 1.6-cm/0.63-in plain tip (#808) with the choux paste. Pipe the paste into 3.2-cm/1.25-in mounds with 2.5-cm/1-in spacing on the baking mat or parchment paper [9]. Brush the top with egg wash using a gentle dabbing motion [10]. Place the reserved macadamia cookie disks on top of the piped mounds [11].

9. Bake at 191°C/375°F for about 15 minutes until the choux are puffed up. Reduce the temperature to 177°C/350°F and bake for another 13 minutes until the choux are golden brown. Turn off the oven and leave the choux in the oven undisturbed for another 10 minutes. Remove the baked choux from the oven and let cool completely [12].

Apricot Cream:

1. In a medium-sized bowl, bloom the sheet gelatin in plenty of cold water. If powdered gelatin is used, sprinkle the powder over 25.2 g/0.89 oz cold water in the bowl. Let the gelatin bloom for at least 10 minutes before using.

2. Combine the apricot puree and sugar in a medium-sized stainless steel saucepan. Mix well with a balloon whisk [13]. Bring the mixture to 71°C/160°F over medium-high heat. Let cool slightly.

3. Meanwhile, squeeze excess water out of the bloomed sheet gelatin and add the gelatin to the apricot mixture [14]. If powdered gelatin is used, add the entire contents to the apricot mixture. Stir to combine. Cover the surface of the apricot jelly with plastic wrap. Let cool completely.

4. In a stand mixer fitted with a whisk attachment, whisk the mascarpone cheese until smooth [15]. Gradually add the apricot jelly and whisk until the mixture is smooth and homogenous.

5. Whisk the chilled heavy cream to stiff peaks using a mixer or by hand. Gently fold the whipped cream into the apricot-mascarpone cheese mixture until well combined [16]. Reserve the cream in the refrigerator until ready to use.

Assembly and Decoration:

1. Use a 1-cm/0.38-in fine star tip (#864) to punch a hole in the bottom of each chou [17].

2. Fill a large pastry bag (45.7-cm/18-in) fitted with a 0.8-cm/0.31-in plain tip (#803) with the apricot cream. Pipe the cream into each chou through the hole in the bottom [18].

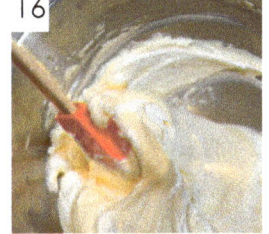

PISTACHIO AND CHERRY

The classic pairing of pistachio and cherry takes center stage in this "not-so-classic" chou creation. Here the pistachio choux are filled with cherry chocolate ganache and adorned with preserved cherries. Be sure to make the cherry chocolate ganache at least a day in advance.

Yield: about 32 5-cm/2-in choux

INGREDIENTS

Cherry Chocolate Ganache:

170 g/6 oz white chocolate couverture, chopped

250 g/8.8 oz cherry puree

300 g/10.6 oz heavy whipping cream

Pistachio Crumble Cookie Topping:

50 g/1.8 oz raw pistachio nuts

50 g/1.8 oz all-purpose flour

50 g/1.8 oz light brown sugar

Pinch of salt

50 g/1.8 oz unsalted butter cubes, at room temperature

Green gel food coloring (optional)

Pistachio Choux:

120 g/4.2 oz all-purpose flour

180 g/6.3 oz distilled water

2 g/0.071 oz (¼ tsp) kosher salt or fine sea salt

5 g/0.18 oz (1 tsp) granulated sugar

Cherry Chocolate Ganache:

1. Place the white chocolate pieces in a mixing bowl. Gently melt the chocolate using a double-boiler. Stir occasionally to allow even heating. Remove the chocolate from the double-boiler when about 75% of the chocolate is melted. Reserve.

2. Boil the cherry puree and cream in a saucepan [1]. Pour the mixture over the chocolate [2]. Wait 1 minute, and then stir the mixture until it is velvety smooth [3].

3. Cover the surface of the soft ganache cream with plastic wrap. Allow the cherry-chocolate ganache to set in the refrigerator overnight.

Pistachio Crumble Cookie Topping:

1. Process the raw pistachio nuts in a food processor for a few seconds. Add the flour, light brown sugar, and salt [4].

2. Pulse the food processor a few times to evenly distribute the ingredients.

3. Add the softened butter pieces and food coloring if used. Pulse the machine a few more times until a smooth dough forms [5]. Do not over-mix.

4. Place the dough between two pieces of plastic wrap and flatten the dough slightly. Chill for 2 hours in the refrigerator.

5. Roll out the dough between two pieces of parchment paper to 2-mm/0.08-in thick [6]. Chill the dough in the refrigerator for about 45 minutes or in the freezer for about 10 minutes.

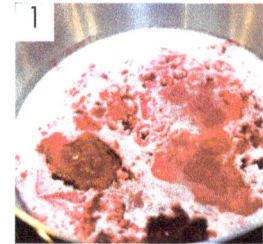

80 g/2.8 oz roasted pistachio oil

200 g/7.1 oz whole eggs (about 4 eggs)

1 whole egg for egg wash

Assembly and Decoration:

200 g/7.1 oz heavy whipping cream

Morello cherries in syrup or brandy (optional)

Powdered sugar

6. Remove the chilled dough from the refrigerator or freezer. Use a 2.8-cm/1.1-in round pastry cutter to cut out circular disks from the dough [7]. Return the cookie disks to the refrigerator or freezer until ready to use.

Pistachio Choux:

1. Sift the flour onto a piece of parchment paper. Transfer the sifted flour to a bowl and reserve.

2. Combine the water, salt, sugar, and pistachio oil in a large stainless steel saucepan; heat the mixture over medium-high heat [8].

3. When the mixture comes to a boil, remove the saucepan from heat. Carefully whisk the sifted flour into the mixture [9]. When all the flour is incorporated into the liquid, shake off lumps of dough from the whisk and switch to a spatula or wooden spoon.

4. Return the saucepan to medium-low heat. Stir the paste using a folding motion to remove any remaining small lumps of flour. Continue to cook for 2 to 3 minutes; stir constantly, using a folding motion to bring the dough pieces together, until a smooth and thick paste is obtained [10].

5. Transfer the dough to a mixer bowl. Attach the bowl to a mixer fitted with a paddle attachment. Mix the dough at medium speed for 10 to 15 seconds to release the steam.

6. Add the eggs one at a time while continuing to mix on medium speed. Make sure each egg is incorporated before adding additional eggs. Scrape down the sides of the mixer bowl with a spatula if necessary. Increase the mixer speed to high. Mix for 10 to 20 seconds or until a smooth paste forms.

7. Meanwhile, line a half-sheet baking pan with a silicone baking mat or parchment paper. Preheat the oven to 191°C/375°F.

8. Fill a large pastry bag (45.7-cm/18-in) fitted with a 1.6-cm/0.63-in plain tip (#808) with the choux paste. Pipe the paste into 3.2-cm/1.25-in mounds with 2.5-cm/1-in spacing on the baking mat or parchment paper [11]. Brush the top with egg wash using a gentle dabbing motion [12]. Place the reserved pistachio cookie disks on top of the piped mounds [13].

9. Bake at 191°C/375°F for about 15 minutes until the choux are puffed up. Reduce the temperature to 177°C/350°F and bake for another 13 minutes until the choux are golden brown. Turn off the oven and leave the choux in the oven undisturbed for another 10 minutes. Remove the baked choux from the oven and let cool completely [14].

Assembly and Decoration:

1. Using a serrated knife, cut off the top ⅓ of each chou and reserve the cap [15].

2. Combine the cherry-chocolate ganache with the fresh cream in a mixer bowl. Whisk the mixture in a stand mixer fitted with a whisk attachment until stiff peaks form [16].

3. Fill a large pastry bag (45.7-cm/18-in) fitted with a 0.79-cm/0.31-in closed star tip (#843) with the cherry-chocolate cream. Pipe the cream into the bottom portion of each chou [17].

4. Arrange the preserved cherries on top if desired [18]. Pipe more cream [19]. Placed the reserved cap on top of the cream [20]. Dust the top with powdered sugar [21].

HAZELNUT, LEMON, AND BASIL

The hazelnut chou topped with hazelnut crumbles is an absolute delight on its own. The addition of rich, luscious lemon-mascarpone cream makes this dessert even more alluring, but it is the essence of fresh basil that makes it unforgettable.

Yield: about 30 6.4-cm/2.5-in mini éclairs

Ingredients

Hazelnut Crumble Topping:

50 g/1.8 oz raw hazelnuts

50 g/1.8 oz all-purpose flour

50 g/1.8 oz light brown sugar

Pinch of salt

50 g/1.8 oz unsalted butter cubes, chilled

Hazelnut Mini Éclairs:

120 g/4.2 oz all-purpose flour

180 g/6.3 oz distilled water

2 g/0.071 oz (¼ tsp) kosher salt or fine sea salt

5 g/0.18 oz (1 tsp) granulated sugar

80 g/2.8 oz roasted hazelnut oil

200 g/7.1 oz whole eggs (about 4 eggs)

1 whole egg for egg wash

Lemon Basil Cream:

120 g/4.2 oz whole eggs

100 g/3.5 oz granulated sugar

Hazelnut Crumble Topping:

1. Process the raw hazelnuts in a food processor for a few seconds [1]. Add the flour, light brown sugar, and salt.

2. Pulse the food processor a few times to evenly distribute the ingredients.

3. Add the chilled butter pieces [2]. Pulse the machine a few more times until a crumbly consistency is obtained. Do not over-mix.

4. Place the dough pieces on a baking tray. Break the larger pieces into pea-sized pieces [3]. Chill the crumbles in the refrigerator.

Hazelnut Mini Éclairs:

1. Sift the flour onto a piece of parchment paper. Transfer the sifted flour to a bowl and reserve.

2. Combine the water, salt, sugar, and hazelnut oil in a large stainless steel saucepan [4]; heat the mixture over medium-high heat.

3. When the mixture comes to a boil, remove the saucepan from heat. Carefully whisk the sifted flour into the mixture [5]. When all the flour is incorporated into the liquid, shake off lumps of dough from the whisk and switch to a spatula or wooden spoon.

4. Return the saucepan to medium-low heat. Stir the paste using a folding motion to remove any remaining small lumps of flour. Continue to cook for 2 to 3

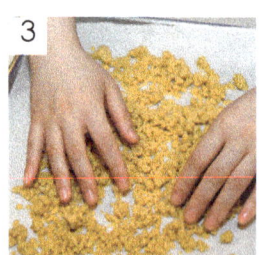

100 g/3.5 oz fresh lemon juice

15 g/0.53 oz lemon zest

8 fresh basil leaves, coarsely chopped

50 g/1.8 oz unsalted butter

150 g/5.3 oz mascarpone cheese, at room temperature

200 g/7.1 oz heavy whipping cream

minutes; stir constantly, using a folding motion to bring the dough pieces together, until a smooth and thick paste is obtained [6].

5. Transfer the dough to a mixer bowl. Attach the bowl to a mixer fitted with a paddle attachment. Mix the dough at medium speed for 10 to 15 seconds to release the steam [7].

6. Add the eggs one at a time while continuing to mix on medium speed [8]. Make sure each egg is incorporated before adding additional eggs. Scrape down the sides of the mixer bowl with a spatula if necessary. Increase the mixer speed to high. Mix for 10 to 20 seconds or until a smooth paste forms.

7. Meanwhile, line a half-sheet baking pan with a silicone baking mat or parchment paper.

8. Preheat the oven to 191°C/375°F. Fill a large pastry bag (45.7-cm/18-in) fitted with a 1.1-cm/0.44-in fine star tip (#865) with the choux paste. Pipe the paste into 6.4-cm/2.5-in logs with 2.5-cm/1-in spacing on the baking mat or parchment paper [9]. Brush the top with egg wash using a gentle dabbing motion [10]. Sprinkle the reserved hazelnut crumbles on top [11].

9. Bake at 191°C/375°F for about 15 minutes until the éclairs are puffed up. Reduce the temperature to 177°C/350°F and bake for another 15 minutes until the éclairs are golden brown. Turn off the oven and leave the éclairs in the oven undisturbed for another 10 minutes. Remove the baked éclairs from the oven and let cool completely [12].

Lemon Basil Cream:

1. Combine eggs, sugar, lemon juice, lemon zest, and basil leaves in a medium-sized stainless steel saucepan. Heat the mixture over medium heat.

2. Gently whisk the mixture to allow even heating [13]. Cook the mixture to 85°C/185°F and remove the pan from the heat. Take care not to over-heat the mixture; otherwise, the eggs in the mixture will coagulate.

3. Add the butter and stir to combine. Pass the mixture through a fine mesh strainer [14]. Cover the surface of the lemon-basil curd with plastic wrap. Let cool completely.

4. In a stand mixer fitted with a whisk attachment, whisk the mascarpone cheese and lemon-basil curd until smooth [15].

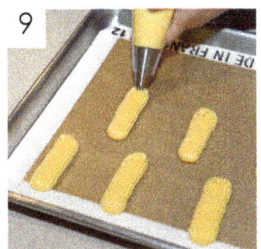

5. Whisk the chilled heavy cream to stiff peaks using a mixer or by hand. Gently fold the whipped cream into the lemon-basil curd and mascarpone cheese mixture until well combined [16]. Reserve the cream in the refrigerator until ready to use.

Assembly and Decoration:

1. Use a 1-cm/0.38-in fine star tip (#864) to punch a hole in the bottom of each éclair [17].

2. Fill a large pastry bag (45.7-cm/18-in) fitted with a 0.8-cm/0.31-in plain tip (#803) with the lemon basil cream. Pipe the cream into each éclair through the hole in the bottom [18].

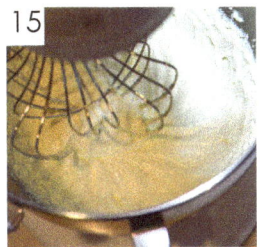 

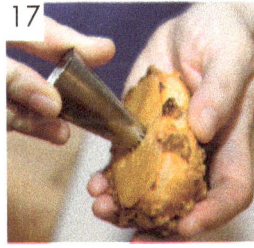 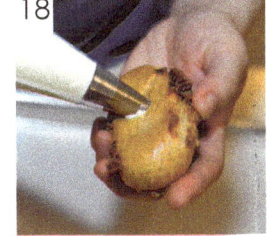

3. HERBS & SPICES

SPICES AND COFFEE

Forget about doughnuts, try these delightful little morsels instead. Intense coffee-flavored cream filling with just a hint of cardamom and cinnamon, this is the perfect snack for your coffee break. You can use ready-made fondant, but if you choose to make it, be sure to make the fondant in advance.

Yield: about 50 3.8-cm/1.5-in mini choux

INGREDIENTS

Pastry Fondant (makes about 600 g/21.2 oz fondant):

500 g/17.6 oz granulated sugar

100 g/3.5 oz distilled water

100 g/3.5 oz glucose syrup

Spice Choux:

120 g/4.2 oz all-purpose flour

100 g/3.5 oz distilled water

100 g/3.5 oz whole milk

2 g/0.071 oz (¼ tsp) kosher salt or fine sea salt

5 g/0.18 oz (1 tsp) granulated sugar

0.5 g/0.018 oz (¼ tsp) powdered cardamom

1 g/0.035 oz (½ tsp) powdered cinnamon

80 g/2.8 oz unsalted butter

200 g/7.1 oz whole eggs (about 4 eggs)

1 whole egg for egg wash

Coffee Mousseline Cream:

60 g/2.1 oz egg yolks

Pastry Fondant (makes about 600 g/21.2 oz fondant):

1. Combine the sugar and water in a medium-sized stainless steel saucepan. Heat the mixture over medium heat. Stir constantly with a spatula until the sugar is dissolved.

2. When the sugar syrup comes to a boil, stir in the glucose syrup [1]. Bring the mixture back to a boil.

3. Insert a candy thermometer and stop stirring. Increase the heat to medium-high. Continue to cook the sugar; brush down the sides of the pan with a pastry brush dipped in cold water to prevent sugar crystals from forming.

4. Cook the sugar until it reaches 118°C/244°F. Let cool slightly. Pour the syrup into a food processor [2] and cover the food processor bowl tightly with plastic wrap.

5. Let the syrup cool to 80°C/176°F. Turn on the food processor. Mix until the syrup turns opaque, white, and glossy [3].

6. Immediately transfer the white fondant into a plastic bag or other container. Cover and let it rest at room temperature overnight before using it. The fondant will become softer and more pliable

Spice Choux:

1. Sift the flour onto a piece of parchment paper. Transfer the sifted flour to a bowl and reserve.

40 g/1.4 oz granulated sugar (A)

23 g/0.81 oz cornstarch

220 g/7.8 oz whole milk

80 g/2.8 oz espresso coffee

35 g/1.2 oz granulated sugar (B)

20 g/0.71 oz unsalted butter (A), at room temperature

150 g/5.3 oz unsalted butter (B), at room temperature

Assembly and Decoration:

45 g/1.6 oz granulated sugar

35 g/1.2 oz espresso coffee

300 g/10.6 oz pastry fondant

2. Combine the water, milk, salt, sugar, cardamom, cinnamon, and butter in a large stainless steel saucepan; heat the mixture over medium-high heat [4].

3. When the mixture comes to a boil, remove the saucepan from heat. Carefully whisk the sifted flour into the mixture [5]. When all the flour is incorporated into the liquid, shake off lumps of dough from the whisk and switch to a spatula or wooden spoon.

4. Return the saucepan to medium-low heat. Stir the paste using a folding motion to remove any remaining small lumps of flour [6]. Continue to cook for 2 to 3 minutes; stir constantly, using a folding motion to bring the dough pieces together, until a smooth and thick paste is obtained.

5. Transfer the dough to a mixer bowl. Attach the bowl to a mixer fitted with a paddle attachment. Mix the dough at medium speed for 10 to 15 seconds to release the steam.

6. Add the eggs one at a time while continuing to mix on medium speed [7]. Make sure each egg is incorporated before adding additional eggs. Scrape down the sides of the mixer bowl with a spatula if necessary. Increase the mixer speed to high. Mix for 10 to 20 seconds or until a smooth paste forms.

7. Meanwhile, line a half-sheet baking pan with a silicone baking mat or parchment paper. Preheat the oven to 191°C/375°F.

8. Fill a large pastry bag (45.7-cm/18-in) fitted with a 1.3-cm/0.5-in plain tip (#806) with the choux paste. Pipe the paste into 2.5-cm/1-in mounds with 2.5-cm/1-in spacing on the baking mat or parchment paper [8]. Brush the top with egg wash using a gentle dabbing motion.

9. Bake at 191°C/375°F for about 13 minutes until the choux are puffed up. Reduce the temperature to 177°C/350°F and bake for another 12 minutes until the choux are golden brown. Turn off the oven and leave the choux in the oven undisturbed for another 6 minutes. Remove the baked choux from the oven and let cool completely [9].

Coffee Mousseline Cream:

1. Combine egg yolks, sugar (A), and cornstarch in a stainless steel mixing bowl. Mix well with a balloon whisk. Set aside.

2. Place the milk, coffee, and sugar (B) in a medium-sized stainless steel saucepan. Heat the milk mixture over medium-high heat. Remove from heat when it comes to a boil.

3. Pour about half of the hot liquid into the reserved egg yolk mixture while whisking vigorously [10]. Pour the mixture back into the pan. Cook the mixture over

medium-low heat while whisking constantly for 1 to 2 minutes until the mixture thickens [11]. Let cool slightly. Stir in the softened butter (A) and mix well.

4. Cover the surface of the coffee pastry cream with plastic wrap. Let cool to room temperature.

5. Place the coffee pastry cream in a mixer bowl. Beat with a stand mixer fitted with a wire whisk attachment on medium-high speed until the cream is smooth.

6. Reduce the mixer speed to medium-low and whisk in the softened butter (B) in small increments. Make sure each addition of butter is thoroughly incorporated before adding more. Scrape down the sides of the bowl with a spatula if necessary.

7. Once all the butter is incorporated, adjust the mixer speed to medium-high. Continue to beat for a few more minutes until the cream is light and fluffy [12]. Reserve.

Assembly and Decoration:

1. Use a 1-cm/0.38-in fine star tip (#864) to punch a hole in the bottom of each chou [13].

2. Fill a large pastry bag (45.7-cm/18-in) fitted with a 0.8-cm/0.31-in plain tip (#803) with the coffee mousseline cream. Pipe the cream into each chou through the hole in the bottom [14].

3. To make the syrup for the fondant glaze, combine the sugar and coffee in a medium-sized saucepan. Bring the mixture to a boil and remove from heat. Let the coffee syrup cool slightly.

4. Combine the coffee syrup and pastry fondant in a medium-sized mixing bowl [15]. Gently heat the mixture over a double-boiler or in a microwave until the mixture reaches 37°C/98.6°F. Stir to combine. Do not heat the mixture hotter than 50°C/122°F.

5. Dip the filled chou into the coffee fondant glaze [16]. Gently shake off excess glaze and place the chou bottom-side down on a piece of parchment paper. Repeat until all the choux are glazed.

LEMONGRASS AND STRAWBERRY

Lemongrass-flavored choux filled with light, refreshing lemongrass cream is paired with aromatic strawberry-balsamic jam. This is the perfect summertime dessert. The lemongrass chocolate ganache should be made in advance, preferably the day before.

Yield: about 30 6.4-cm/2.5-in mini éclairs

INGREDIENTS

Lemongrass Chocolate Ganache:

400 g/14.1 oz heavy whipping cream

70 g/2.5 oz chopped lemongrass

120 g/4.2 oz white chocolate couverture, chopped

Lemongrass Mini Éclairs:

120 g/4.2 oz all-purpose flour

90 g/3.2 oz grapeseed oil

40 g/1.4 oz chopped lemongrass

180 g/6.3 oz distilled water

2 g/0.071 oz (¼ tsp) kosher salt or fine sea salt

5 g/0.18 oz (1 tsp) granulated sugar

200 g/7.1 oz whole eggs (about 4 eggs)

1 whole egg for egg wash

Strawberry and Balsamic Jam:

5 g/0.18 oz gelatin sheet (silver grade) or 4.2 g/0.15 oz powdered gelatin + 25.2 g/0.89 oz cold water

90 g/3.2 oz granulated sugar

Lemongrass Chocolate Ganache:

1. Combine the cream and chopped lemongrass in a medium-sized stainless steel saucepan [1]. Bring the mixture to a boil. Remove from heat. Cover the pan and allow the mixture to infuse for about 15 minutes.

2. Meanwhile, place the white chocolate in a mixing bowl. Gently melt the chocolate using a double-boiler. Stir occasionally to allow even heating. Remove the chocolate from the double-boiler when about 75% of the chocolate is melted. Reserve.

3. Bring the infused cream back to a boil and strain over the melted chocolate using a fine mesh strainer [2]. Wait 1 minute and then stir the mixture until it is velvety smooth.

4. Cover the surface of the soft ganache with plastic wrap. Allow the ganache cream to set in the refrigerator overnight.

Lemongrass Mini Éclairs:

1. Sift the flour onto a piece of parchment paper. Transfer the sifted flour to a bowl and reserve.

2. Heat the oil in a saucepan to about 191°C/375°F. Add the chopped lemongrass into pan and stir for a few seconds [3]. Remove from heat and let the oil cool completely. Remove the lemongrass pieces from the oil using a fine mesh strainer.

3. Combine the water, salt, sugar, and lemongrass infused oil in a large stainless steel saucepan; heat the mixture over medium-high heat [4].

2 g/0.071 oz (½ tsp) powdered pectin NH

250 g/8.8 oz strawberry puree

5 g/0.18 oz (1 tsp) aged balsamic vinegar

Assembly and Decoration:

120 g/4.2 oz heavy whipping cream

Green gel food coloring

Fresh strawberries

4. When the mixture comes to a boil, remove the saucepan from heat. Carefully whisk the sifted flour into the mixture [5]. When all the flour is incorporated into the liquid, shake off lumps of dough from the whisk and switch to a spatula or wooden spoon.

5. Return the saucepan to medium-low heat. Stir the paste using a folding motion to remove any remaining small lumps of flour. Continue to cook for 2 to 3 minutes; stir constantly, using a folding motion to bring the dough pieces together, until a smooth and thick paste is obtained [6].

6. Transfer the dough to a mixer bowl. Attach the bowl to a mixer fitted with a paddle attachment. Mix the dough at medium speed for 10 to 15 seconds to release the steam.

7. Add the eggs one at a time while continuing to mix on medium speed [7]. Make sure each egg is incorporated before adding additional eggs. Scrape down the sides of the mixer bowl with a spatula if necessary. Increase the mixer speed to high. Mix for 10 to 20 seconds or until a smooth paste forms [8].

8. Meanwhile, line a half-sheet baking pan with a silicone baking mat or parchment paper.

9. Preheat the oven to 191°C/375°F. Fill a large pastry bag (45.7-cm/18-in) fitted with a 1.1-cm/0.44-in fine star tip (#865) with the choux paste. Pipe the paste into 6.4-cm/2.5-in logs with 2.5-cm/1-in spacing on the baking mat or parchment paper [9]. Brush the top with egg wash using a gentle dabbing motion [10].

10. Bake at 191°C/375°F for about 15 minutes until the éclairs are puffed up. Reduce the temperature to 177°C/350°F and bake for another 15 minutes until the éclairs are golden brown. Turn off the oven and leave the éclairs in the oven undisturbed for another 10 minutes. Remove the baked éclairs from the oven and let cool completely.

Strawberry and Balsamic Jam:

1. In a medium-sized bowl, bloom the sheet gelatin in plenty of cold water. If powdered gelatin is used, sprinkle the powder over 25.2 g/0.89 oz cold water in the bowl. Let the gelatin bloom for at least 10 minutes before using.

2. Combine half the sugar and pectin in a mixing bowl. Mix thoroughly and reserve.

3. In a medium-sized stainless steel saucepan, combine the remaining sugar and strawberry puree. Bring the mixture to a boil over medium-high heat. Stir in the sugar-pectin mixture [11]. Bring the mixture back to a boil and reduce the heat to medium-low. Stir constantly and cook for another 5 minutes. Remove from heat. Stir in the balsamic vinegar [12].

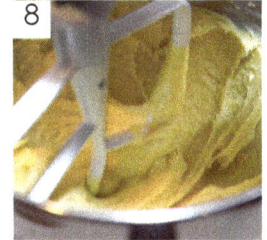

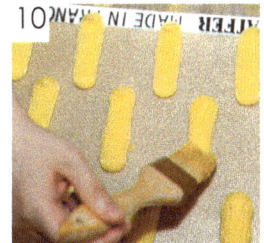

4. Squeeze excess water out of the bloomed sheet gelatin and add the gelatin to the strawberry mixture [13]. If powdered gelatin is used, add the entire contents to the strawberry mixture. Stir to combine.

5. Cover the surface of the strawberry jam with plastic wrap. Allow the jam to cool completely and reserve in the refrigerator.

Assembly and Decoration:

1. Using a serrated knife, cut off the top ⅓ of each éclair and reserve the top [14].

2. Combine the lemongrass-chocolate ganache with the fresh cream in a mixer bowl. Add a drop of green food coloring if desired. Whisk the mixture in a stand mixer fitted with a whisk attachment until stiff peaks form [15].

3. Fill a large pastry bag (45.7-cm/18-in) fitted with a 1-cm/0.38-in closed star tip (#844) with the lemongrass-chocolate cream. Pipe the cream into the bottom portion of each éclair [16].

 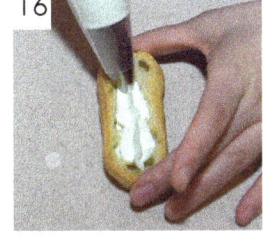

4. Fill a large pastry bag (45.7-cm/18-in) fitted with a 0.64-cm/0.25-in plain tip (#802) with the strawberry-balsamic jam. Pipe the jam on top of the cream [17].

5. Place the reserved éclair top, glossy side down, on top of the jam [18]. Pipe more lemongrass-chocolate cream [19]. Arrange fresh strawberry pieces on top of the cream [20].

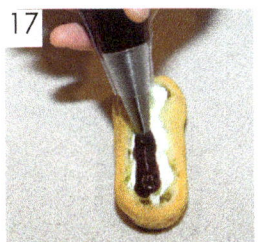 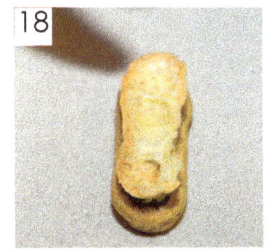

HERBS & SPICES   63

ORANGE BLOSSOM

Three orange ingredients are used in this recipe—fresh oranges, orange blossom honey, and orange blossom water. The orange zest and juice bring freshness whereas the orange blossom honey and water add a pungent orange bouquet. No doubt, this is an orange lover's dream dessert.

Be sure to make the fondant at least a day in advance; you can save the leftover fondant for other uses.

Yield: about 50 3.8-cm/1.5-in mini choux

Ingredients

Pastry Fondant (makes about 600 g/21.2 oz fondant):

500 g/17.6 oz granulated sugar

100 g/3.5 oz distilled water

100 g/3.5 oz glucose syrup

Orange Choux:

120 g/4.2 oz all-purpose flour

100 g/3.5 oz distilled water

100 g/3.5 oz whole milk

2 g/0.071 oz (¼ tsp) kosher salt or fine sea salt

5 g/0.18 oz (1 tsp) granulated sugar

80 g/2.8 oz unsalted butter

Zest of one orange

200 g/7.1 oz whole eggs (about 4 eggs)

1 whole egg for egg wash

Orange Blossom Cream:

5 g/0.18 oz gelatin sheet (silver grade) or 4.2 g/0.15 oz powdered gelatin + 25.2 g/0.89 oz cold water

Pastry Fondant (makes about 600 g/21.2 oz fondant):

1. Combine the sugar and water in a medium-sized stainless steel saucepan. Heat the mixture over medium heat. Stir constantly with a spatula until the sugar is dissolved.

2. When the sugar syrup comes to a boil, stir in the glucose syrup [1]. Bring the mixture back to a boil.

3. Insert a candy thermometer and stop stirring. Increase the heat to medium-high. Continue to cook the sugar; brush down the sides of the pan with a pastry brush dipped in cold water to prevent sugar crystals from forming.

4. Cook the sugar until it reaches 118°C/244°F. Let cool slightly. Pour the syrup into a food processor [2] and cover the food processor bowl tightly with plastic wrap.

5. Let the syrup cool to 80°C/176°F. Turn on the food processor. Mix until the syrup turns opaque, white, and glossy [3].

6. Immediately transfer the white fondant into a plastic bag or other container. Cover and let it rest at room temperature overnight before using it. The fondant will become softer and more pliable

Orange Choux:

1. Sift the flour onto a piece of parchment paper. Transfer the sifted flour to a bowl and reserve.

150 g/5.3 oz fresh orange juice

20 g/0.71 oz (1 Tbsp) orange blossom honey

Zest of two oranges

150 g/5.3 oz mascarpone cheese, at room temperature

15 g/0.53 oz (1 Tbsp) orange blossom water

200 g/7.1 oz heavy whipping cream

Assembly and Decoration:

30 g/1.1 oz granulated sugar

35 g/1.2 oz fresh orange juice

5 g/0.18 oz (1 tsp) orange blossom water

300 g/10.6 oz pastry fondant

Orange gel food coloring

2. Combine the water, milk, salt, sugar, butter, and orange zest in a large stainless steel saucepan; heat the mixture over medium-high heat [4].

3. When the mixture comes to a boil, remove the saucepan from heat. Carefully whisk the sifted flour into the mixture. When all the flour is incorporated into the liquid, shake off lumps of dough from the whisk and switch to a spatula or wooden spoon.

4. Return the saucepan to medium-low heat. Stir the paste using a folding motion to remove any remaining small lumps of flour. Continue to cook for 2 to 3 minutes; stir constantly, using a folding motion to bring the dough pieces together, until a smooth and thick paste is obtained [5].

5. Transfer the dough to a mixer bowl. Attach the bowl to a mixer fitted with a paddle attachment. Mix the dough at medium speed for 10 to 15 seconds to release the steam [6].

6. Add the eggs one at a time while continuing to mix on medium speed [7]. Make sure each egg is incorporated before adding additional eggs. Scrape down the sides of the mixer bowl with a spatula if necessary. Increase the mixer speed to high. Mix for 10 to 20 seconds or until a smooth paste forms.

7. Meanwhile, line a half-sheet baking pan with a silicone baking mat or parchment paper. Preheat the oven to 191°C/375°F.

8. Fill a large pastry bag (45.7-cm/18-in) fitted with a 1.3-cm/0.5-in plain tip (#806) with the choux paste. Pipe the paste into 2.5-cm/1-in mounds with 2.5-cm/1-in spacing on the baking mat or parchment paper. Brush the top with egg wash using a gentle dabbing motion [8].

9. Bake at 191°C/375°F for about 13 minutes until the choux are puffed up. Reduce the temperature to 177°C/350°F and bake for another 13 minutes until the choux are golden brown. Turn off the oven and leave the choux in the oven undisturbed for another 8 minutes. Remove the baked choux from the oven and let cool completely [9].

Orange Blossom Cream:

1. In a medium-sized bowl, bloom the sheet gelatin in plenty of cold water. If powdered gelatin is used, sprinkle the powder over 25.2 g/0.89 oz cold water in the bowl. Let the gelatin bloom for at least 10 minutes before using.

2. Combine the fresh orange juice, honey, and orange zest in a medium-sized stainless steel saucepan. Mix well with a balloon whisk [10]. Bring the mixture to 71°C/160°F over medium-high heat. Let cool slightly.

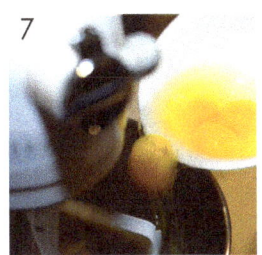

3. Meanwhile, squeeze excess water out of the bloomed sheet gelatin and add the gelatin to the orange mixture [11]. If powdered gelatin is used, add the entire contents to the orange mixture. Stir to combine. Cover the surface of the orange jelly with plastic wrap. Let cool completely.

4. In a stand mixer fitted with a whisk attachment, whisk the mascarpone cheese and orange blossom water until smooth. Gradually add the orange jelly and whisk until the mixture is smooth and homogenous [12].

5. Whisk the chilled heavy cream to stiff peaks using a mixer or by hand. Gently fold the whipped cream into the orange-mascarpone cheese mixture until well combined [13]. Chill the cream in the refrigerator for about 2 hours until the cream is set.

Assembly and Decoration:

1. Use a 1-cm/0.38-in fine star tip (#864) to punch a hole in the bottom of each chou [14].

2. Fill a large pastry bag (45.7-cm/18-in) fitted with a 0.8-cm/0.31-in plain tip (#803) with the orange blossom cream. Pipe the cream into each chou through the hole in the bottom [15].

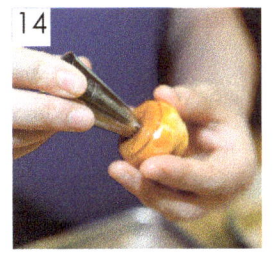

3. To make the syrup for the fondant glaze, combine the sugar and orange juice in a medium-sized saucepan. Bring the mixture to a boil and remove from heat. Let the orange syrup cool slightly.

4. Combine the orange syrup, orange blossom water, pastry fondant, and food coloring in a medium-sized mixing bowl. Gently heat the mixture over a double-boiler or in a microwave until the mixture reaches 37°C/98.6°F. Stir to combine. Do not heat the mixture hotter than 50°C/122°F.

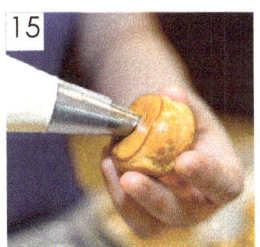

5. Dip the filled chou into the orange fondant glaze [16]. Gently shake off excess glaze and place the chou bottom-side down on a piece of parchment paper. Repeat until all the choux are glazed [17].

HERBS & SPICES

SICHUAN PEPPERCORN AND SESAME

Sichuan peppercorn oil-flavored choux are topped with sesame seeds and crunchy turbinado sugar crystals. The smooth, creamy sesame mousseline cream filling is equally enticing. Served with coffee or tea, this dessert will remind you of your last trip to the bustling spice market.

Yield: about 50 3.8-cm/1.5-in mini choux

INGREDIENTS

Sichuan Peppercorn Choux:

120 g/4.2 oz all-purpose flour

85 g/3 oz grapeseed oil

5 g/0.18 oz (1 Tbsp) whole Sichuan peppercorns

180 g/6.3 oz distilled water

2 g/0.071 oz (¼ tsp) kosher salt or fine sea salt

5 g/0.18 oz (1 tsp) granulated sugar

200 g/7.1 oz whole eggs (about 4 eggs)

1 whole egg for egg wash

Mixed-color sesame seeds

Turbinado sugar

Sesame Mousseline Cream:

60 g/2.1 oz egg yolks

40 g/1.4 oz granulated sugar (A)

23 g/0.81 oz cornstarch

300 g/10.6 oz whole milk

35 g/1.2 oz granulated sugar (B)

Sichuan Peppercorn Choux:

1. Sift the flour onto a piece of parchment paper. Transfer the sifted flour to a bowl and reserve.

2. Heat the oil in a saucepan to about 191°C/375°F. Add Sichuan peppercorns into pan and stir for about a minute. Remove from heat and let the oil cool completely. Remove the peppercorns from the oil using a fine mesh strainer.

3. Combine the water, salt, sugar, and Sichuan peppercorn infused oil in a large stainless steel saucepan; heat the mixture over medium-high heat [1].

4. When the mixture comes to a boil, remove the saucepan from heat. Carefully whisk the sifted flour into the mixture [2]. When all the flour is incorporated into the liquid, shake off lumps of dough from the whisk and switch to a spatula or wooden spoon.

5. Return the saucepan to medium-low heat. Stir the paste using a folding motion to remove any remaining small lumps of flour. Continue to cook for 2 to 3 minutes; stir constantly, using a folding motion to bring the dough pieces together, until a smooth and thick paste is obtained [3].

6. Transfer the dough to a mixer bowl. Attach the bowl to a mixer fitted with a paddle attachment. Mix the dough at medium speed for 10 to 15 seconds to release the steam.

7. Add the eggs one at a time while continuing to mix on medium speed [4]. Make sure each egg is incorporated before adding additional eggs. Scrape down the

120 g/4.2 oz natural sesame paste

180 g/6.3 oz unsalted butter, at room temperature

sides of the mixer bowl with a spatula if necessary. Increase the mixer speed to high. Mix for 10 to 20 seconds or until a smooth paste forms.

8. Meanwhile, line a half-sheet baking pan with a silicone baking mat or parchment paper. Preheat the oven to 191°C/375°F.

9. Fill a large pastry bag (45.7-cm/18-in) fitted with a 1.3-cm/0.5-in plain tip (#806) with the choux paste. Pipe the paste into 2.5-cm/1-in mounds with 2.5-cm/1-in spacing on the baking mat or parchment paper [5]. Brush the top with egg wash using a gentle dabbing motion. Sprinkle sesame seeds and Turbinado sugar on top [6].

10. Bake at 191°C/375°F for about 13 minutes until the choux are puffed up. Reduce the temperature to 177°C/350°F and bake for another 12 minutes until the choux are golden brown. Turn off the oven and leave the choux in the oven undisturbed for another 6 minutes. Remove the baked choux from the oven and let cool completely [7].

Sesame Mousseline Cream:

1. Combine egg yolks, sugar (A), and cornstarch in a stainless steel mixing bowl. Mix well with a balloon whisk [8]. Set aside.

2. Place the milk and sugar (B) in a medium-sized stainless steel saucepan. Heat the milk mixture over medium-high heat. Remove from heat when it comes to a boil.

3. Pour about half of the hot liquid into the reserved egg yolk mixture while whisking vigorously [9]. Pour the mixture back into the pan. Cook the mixture over medium-low heat while whisking constantly for 1 to 2 minutes until the mixture thickens [10].

4. Cover the surface of the pastry cream with plastic wrap. Let cool to room temperature.

5. Place the pastry cream and sesame paste in a mixer bowl. Beat with a stand mixer fitted with a wire whisk attachment on medium-high speed until the cream is smooth.

6. Reduce the mixer speed to medium-low and whisk in the softened butter in small increments [11]. Make sure each addition of butter is thoroughly incorporated before adding more. Scrape down the sides of the bowl with a spatula if necessary.

7. Once all the butter is incorporated, adjust the mixer speed to medium-high. Continue to beat for a few more minutes until the cream is light and fluffy. Reserve.

Assembly and Decoration:

1. Use a 1-cm/0.38-in fine star tip (#864) to punch a hole in the bottom of each chou [12, 13].

2. Fill a large pastry bag (45.7-cm/18-in) fitted with a 0.8-cm/0.31-in plain tip (#803) with the sesame mousseline cream. Pipe the cream into each chou through the hole in the bottom [14].

 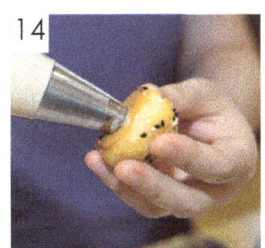

ROSEMARY AND MINT

This is a savory-sweet dessert that offers an interesting herbaceous note. Walnut oil and herb-infused choux are filled with rosemary and mint chocolate cream and covered with walnut and herb crumble toppings. Served with hot chocolate or coffee, this is the ultimate cold-weather comfort dessert.

Be sure to make the herb chocolate cream a day in advance; this will allow it time to set properly.

Yield: about 32 5-cm/2-in choux

INGREDIENTS

Herb Chocolate Cream:

770 g/27.2 oz heavy whipping cream

2 rosemary sprigs

10 small mint leaves

230 g/8.1 oz bittersweet chocolate couverture, chopped

Walnut and Herb Crumble Cookie Topping:

50 g/1.8 oz raw walnuts

1.5 g/0.053 oz (1 tsp) finely chopped rosemary

1 g/0.035 oz (1 tsp) finely chopped mint leaves

50 g/1.8 oz all-purpose flour

50 g/1.8 oz light brown sugar

Pinch of salt

50 g/1.8 oz unsalted butter cubes, at room temperature

Walnut and Herb Choux:

120 g/4.2 oz all-purpose flour

180 g/6.3 oz distilled water

Herb Chocolate Cream:

1. Combine the cream, rosemary, and mint in a medium-sized stainless steel saucepan [1]. Bring the mixture to a boil. Remove from heat. Cover the pan and allow the mixture to infuse for about 15 minutes.

2. Meanwhile, place the dark chocolate in a mixing bowl. Gently melt the chocolate using a double-boiler [2]. Stir occasionally to allow even heating. Remove the chocolate from the double-boiler when about 75% of the chocolate is melted. Reserve.

3. Bring the infused cream back to a boil and strain over the melted chocolate using a fine mesh strainer [3]. Wait 1 minute and then stir the mixture until it is velvety smooth [4].

4. Cover the surface of the soft ganache cream with plastic wrap. Allow the ganache cream to set in the refrigerator overnight.

Walnut and Herb Crumble Cookie Topping:

1. Process the raw walnuts, rosemary, and mint in a food processor for a few seconds [5]. Add the flour, light brown sugar, and salt.

2. Pulse the food processor a few times to evenly distribute the ingredients.

3. Add the softened butter pieces [6]. Pulse the machine a few more times until a smooth dough forms. Do not over-mix.

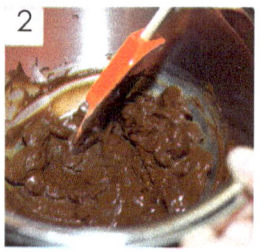

2 g/0.071 oz (¼ tsp) kosher salt or fine sea salt

5 g/0.18 oz (1 tsp) granulated sugar

80 g/2.8 oz walnut oil

1.5 g/0.053 oz (1 tsp) finely chopped rosemary

1 g/0.035 oz (1 tsp) finely chopped mint leaves

200 g/7.1 oz whole eggs (about 4 eggs)

1 whole egg for egg wash

4. Place the dough between two pieces of plastic wrap and flatten the dough slightly. Chill for 2 hours in the refrigerator.

5. Roll out the dough between two pieces of parchment paper to 2-mm/0.08-in thick [7]. Chill the dough in the refrigerator for about 45 minutes or in the freezer for about 10 minutes.

6. Remove the chilled dough from the refrigerator or freezer. Use a 2.8-cm/1.1-in round pastry cutter to cut out circular disks from the dough [8]. Return the cookie disks to the refrigerator or freezer until ready to use.

Walnut and Herb Choux:

1. Sift the flour onto a piece of parchment paper. Transfer the sifted flour to a bowl and reserve.

2. Combine the water, salt, sugar, walnut oil, rosemary, and mint in a large stainless steel saucepan; heat the mixture over medium-high heat [9].

3. When the mixture comes to a boil, remove the saucepan from heat. Carefully whisk the sifted flour into the mixture [10]. When all the flour is incorporated into the liquid, shake off lumps of dough from the whisk and switch to a spatula or wooden spoon.

4. Return the saucepan to medium-low heat. Stir the paste using a folding motion to remove any remaining small lumps of flour. Continue to cook for 2 to 3 minutes; stir constantly, using a folding motion to bring the dough pieces together, until a smooth and thick paste is obtained [11].

5. Transfer the dough to a mixer bowl. Attach the bowl to a mixer fitted with a paddle attachment. Mix the dough at medium speed for 10 to 15 seconds to release the steam.

6. Add the eggs one at a time while continuing to mix on medium speed [12]. Make sure each egg is incorporated before adding additional eggs. Scrape down the sides of the mixer bowl with a spatula if necessary. Increase the mixer speed to high. Mix for 10 to 20 seconds or until a smooth paste forms.

7. Meanwhile, line a half-sheet baking pan with a silicone baking mat or parchment paper. Preheat the oven to 191°C/375°F.

8. Fill a large pastry bag (45.7-cm/18-in) fitted with a 1.6-cm/0.63-in plain tip (#808) with the choux paste. Pipe the paste into 3.2-cm/1.25-in mounds with 2.5-cm/1-in spacing on the baking mat or parchment paper [13]. Brush the top with egg wash using a gentle dabbing motion. Place the reserved walnut and herb cookie disks on top of the piped mounds [14].

9. Bake at 191°C/375°F for about 15 minutes until the choux are puffed up. Reduce the temperature to 177°C/350°F and bake for another 13 minutes until the choux are golden brown. Turn off the oven and leave the choux in the oven undisturbed for another 10 minutes. Remove the baked choux from the oven and let cool completely [15].

Assembly and Decoration:

1. Use a 1-cm/0.38-in fine star tip (#864) to punch a hole in the bottom of each chou [16].

2. Transfer the chilled herb chocolate cream into a mixer bowl. Attach the bowl to a stand mixer fitted with a whisk attachment. Whisk the soft ganache cream on high speed until stiff peaks form [17].

3. Fill a large pastry bag (45.7-cm/18-in) fitted with a 0.8-cm/0.31-in plain tip (#803) with the herb chocolate cream. Pipe the cream into each chou through the hole in the bottom [18].

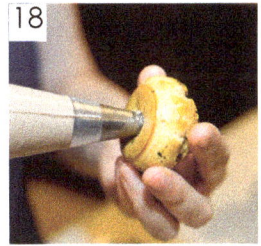

SPICE CHOU-TART

Simple yet stunning, you can showcase all your spice choux creations with this impressive tart. You can substitute the spice choux with other assorted little choux. You can also use alternative flavorings in the Chantilly cream. This tart is the perfect blank canvas for presenting your creations.

Yield: one 20-cm/8-in round tart

INGREDIENTS

Spice Tart Base:

125 g/4.4 oz all-purpose flour

15 g/0.53 oz almond flour

50 g/1.8 oz powdered sugar

0.25 g/0.0088 oz (⅛ tsp) powdered cinnamon

0.25 g /0.0088 oz (⅛ tsp) powdered cardamom powder

Pinch of salt

1 vanilla bean

75 g/2.6 oz unsalted butter cubes, at room temperature

30 g/1.1 oz whole eggs, at room temperature

Almond Chantilly Cream:

100 g/3.5 oz mascarpone cheese

300 g/10.6 oz heavy whipping cream

50 g/1.8 oz granulated sugar

5 g/0.18 oz (1 tsp) almond extract

Assembly and Decoration:

20 to 25 assorted spice choux

Almond slices

Spice Tart Base:

1. Combine the flour, almond flour, powdered sugar, cinnamon, cardamom, and salt in a food processor [1]. Pulse the machine a few times to evenly distribute all dry ingredients.

2. Use a paring knife to split the vanilla bean lengthwise. Scrape off the vanilla seeds using the back of the knife. Add the vanilla seeds and softened butter pieces to the food processor.

3. Pulse the machine a few more times until small pea-sized dough pieces are formed. Add the whole eggs [2] and process for a few seconds until a smooth dough forms [3]. Do not over-mix.

4. Wrap the dough between two pieces of plastic wrap and flatten the dough slightly. Chill in the refrigerator for about 2 hours.

5. Roll out the dough between two pieces of parchment paper to a 2-mm/0.08-in thickness [4]. Chill the dough again in the refrigerator for about 45 minutes or in the freezer for about 8 minutes.

6. Preheat the oven to 177°C/350°F. Remove the chilled dough from the refrigerator or freezer. Dock the dough with a dough docker or fork [5]. Cut out a 20-cm/8-in circle using a 20-cm/8-in round tart ring as a guide [6].

7. Remove the tart ring. Transfer the tart base to a baking pan lined with parchment paper [7]. Bake the tart base for about 18 to 20 minutes until golden brown [8]. Let cool completely.

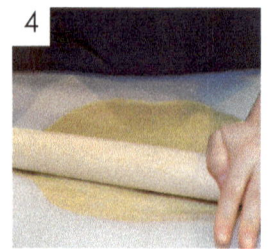

Almond Chantilly Cream:

1. In a mixer bowl, combine the mascarpone cheese, heavy cream, sugar, and almond extract.

2. Attach the mixer bowl to a mixer fitted with a whisk attachment. Whisk the mixture on medium speed until the mixture thickens slightly. Increase the speed to high and whisk the mixture until stiff peaks form. Do not over-beat.

Assembly and Decoration:

1. Fill a large pastry bag (45.7-cm/18-in) fitted with a 1-cm/0.38-in fine star tip (#864) with the almond Chantilly cream. Pipe some cream on the tart base [9].

2. Arrange the spice choux on top of the cream [10]. Pipe more cream around choux, and then place more choux on top [11–13].

3. Sprinkle the spice choux tart with almond slices if desired [14].

Herbs & Spices

4. VEGGIES

**Avocado
Beets
Carrots
Zucchini Doughnuts
Red Pepper & Mango**

AVOCADO

Rich avocado cream is embraced by a crispy thin shell topped with crunchy toasted pumpkin seeds. You can enjoy it on its own or complement it with a refreshing margarita cocktail. Either way, this is a dessert to remember.

Yield: about 30 6.4-cm/2.5-in mini éclairs

INGREDIENTS

Avocado Mini Éclairs:

120 g/4.2 oz all-purpose flour

180 g/6.3 oz distilled water

2 g/0.071 oz (¼ tsp) kosher salt or fine sea salt

5 g/0.18 oz (1 tsp) granulated sugar

80 g/2.8 oz avocado oil

200 g/7.1 oz whole eggs (about 4 eggs)

1 whole egg for egg wash

Raw pumpkin seeds

Avocado Cream:

400 g/14.1 oz ripe avocado flesh

100 g/3.5 oz mascarpone cheese

30 g/1.1 oz (2 Tbsp) fresh lemon juice

50 g/1.8 oz granulated sugar

Zest of one lemon

100 g/3.5 oz heavy whipping cream

Avocado Mini Éclairs:

1. Sift the flour onto a piece of parchment paper. Transfer the sifted flour to a bowl and reserve.

2. Combine the water, salt, sugar, and avocado oil in a large stainless steel saucepan; heat the mixture over medium-high heat [1].

3. When the mixture comes to a boil, remove the saucepan from heat. Carefully whisk the sifted flour into the mixture [2]. When all the flour is incorporated into the liquid, shake off lumps of dough from the whisk and switch to a spatula or wooden spoon.

4. Return the saucepan to medium-low heat. Stir the paste using a folding motion to remove any remaining small lumps of flour. Continue to cook for 2 to 3 minutes; stir constantly, using a folding motion to bring the dough pieces together, until a smooth and thick paste is obtained [3].

5. Transfer the dough to a mixer bowl. Attach the bowl to a mixer fitted with a paddle attachment. Mix the dough at medium speed for 10 to 15 seconds to release the steam.

6. Add the eggs one at a time while continuing to mix on medium speed [4]. Make sure each egg is incorporated before adding additional eggs. Scrape down the sides of the mixer bowl with a spatula if necessary. Increase the mixer speed to high. Mix for 10 to 20 seconds or until a smooth paste forms.

7. Meanwhile, line a half-sheet baking pan with a silicone baking mat or parchment paper.

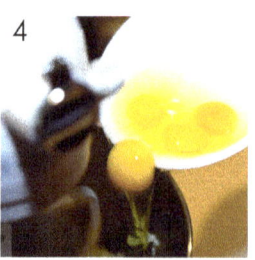

8. Preheat the oven to 191°C/375°F. Fill a large pastry bag (45.7-cm/18-in) fitted with a 1.1-cm/0.44-in fine star tip (#865) with the choux paste. Pipe the paste into 6.4-cm/2.5-in logs with 2.5-cm/1-in spacing on the baking mat or parchment paper [5]. Brush the top with egg wash using a gentle dabbing motion [6]. Sprinkle pumpkin seeds on top [7].

9. Bake at 191°C/375°F for about 15 minutes until the éclairs are puffed up. Reduce the temperature to 177°C/350°F and bake for another 15 minutes until the éclairs are golden brown. Turn off the oven and leave the éclairs in the oven undisturbed for another 10 minutes. Remove the baked éclairs from the oven and let cool completely.

Avocado Cream:

1. In a food processor or blender, combine the avocado flesh, mascarpone cheese, lemon juice, sugar, and lemon zest [8]. Blend the mixture until it is smooth and well combined [9].

2. Whip the chilled heavy cream to stiff peaks. Gently fold about ½ of the whipped cream into the avocado mixture; fold until the mixture is homogenous. Fold in the remaining whipped cream [10]. Reserve the avocado cream in the refrigerator until ready to use.

Assembly and Decoration:

1. Use a 1-cm/0.38-in fine star tip (#864) to punch a hole in the bottom of each éclair [11].

2. Fill a large pastry bag (45.7-cm/18-in) fitted with a 0.8-cm/0.31-in plain tip (#803) with the avocado cream. Pipe the cream into each éclair through the hole in the bottom [12].

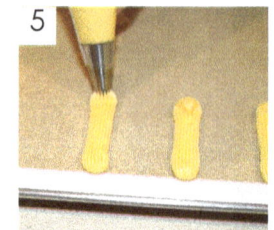

BEETS

Beet juice and olive oil in the choux paste create a unique texture that is light and crispy, and the choux are almost transparent in appearance. The beet and balsamic flavors complement the mascarpone cream perfectly in this exceptional creation.

Yield: about 50 3.8-cm/1.5-in mini choux

INGREDIENTS

Beet Choux:

120 g/4.2 oz all-purpose flour

150 g/5.3 oz distilled water

30 g/1.1 oz fresh beet juice

2 g/0.071 oz (¼ tsp) kosher salt or fine sea salt

5 g/0.18 oz (1 tsp) granulated sugar

80 g/2.8 oz extra-virgin olive oil

200 g/7.1 oz whole eggs (about 4 eggs)

1 whole egg for egg wash

40 g/1.4 oz parmesan cheese, finely grated

Beet and Balsamic Cream:

5 g/0.18 oz gelatin sheet (silver grade) or 4.2 g/0.15 oz powdered gelatin + 25.2 g/0.89 oz cold water

150 g/5.3 oz fresh beet juice

20 g/0.71 oz granulated sugar

20 g/0.71 oz (1 Tbsp) honey

10 g/0.35 oz (2 tsp) aged balsamic vinegar

150 g/5.3 oz mascarpone cheese, at room temperature

200 g/7.1 oz heavy whipping cream

Beet Choux:

1. Sift the flour onto a piece of parchment paper. Transfer the sifted flour to a bowl and reserve.

2. Combine the water, beet juice, salt, sugar, and olive oil in a large stainless steel saucepan; heat the mixture over medium-high heat [1].

3. When the mixture comes to a boil, remove the saucepan from heat. Carefully whisk the sifted flour into the mixture [2]. When all the flour is incorporated into the liquid, shake off lumps of dough from the whisk and switch to a spatula or wooden spoon.

4. Return the saucepan to medium-low heat. Stir the paste using a folding motion to remove any remaining small lumps of flour. Continue to cook for 2 to 3 minutes; stir constantly, using a folding motion to bring the dough pieces together, until a smooth and thick paste is obtained [3].

5. Transfer the dough to a mixer bowl. Attach the bowl to a mixer fitted with a paddle attachment. Mix the dough at medium speed for 10 to 15 seconds to release the steam.

6. Add the eggs one at a time while continuing to mix on medium speed. Make sure each egg is incorporated before adding additional eggs. Scrape down the sides of the mixer bowl with a spatula if necessary. Increase the mixer speed to high. Mix for 10 to 20 seconds or until a smooth paste forms [4].

7. Meanwhile, line a half-sheet baking pan with a silicone baking mat or parchment paper. Preheat the oven to 191°C/375°F.

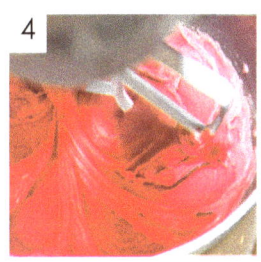

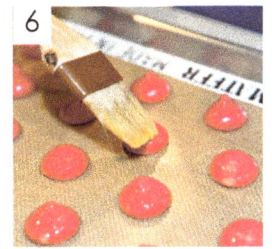

8. Fill a large pastry bag (45.7-cm/18-in) fitted with a 1.3-cm/0.5-in plain tip (#806) with the choux paste. Pipe the paste into 2.5-cm/1-in mounds with 2.5-cm/1-in spacing on the baking mat or parchment paper [5]. Brush the top with egg wash using a gentle dabbing motion [6]. Sprinkle grated cheese on top [7].

9. Bake at 191°C/375°F for about 13 minutes until the choux are puffed up. Reduce the temperature to 177°C/350°F and bake for another 12 minutes until the choux are golden brown. Turn off the oven and leave the choux in the oven undisturbed for another 6 minutes. Remove the baked choux from the oven and let cool completely [8].

Beet and Balsamic Cream:

1. In a medium-sized bowl, bloom the sheet gelatin in plenty of cold water. If powdered gelatin is used, sprinkle the powder over 25.2 g/0.89 oz cold water in the bowl. Let the gelatin bloom for at least 10 minutes before using.

2. Combine the fresh beet juice, sugar, honey, and balsamic vinegar in a medium-sized stainless steel saucepan [9]. Bring the mixture to 71°C/160°F over medium-high heat. Let cool slightly.

3. Meanwhile, squeeze excess water out of the bloomed sheet gelatin and add the gelatin to the beet mixture [10]. If powdered gelatin is used, add the entire contents to the beet mixture. Stir to combine. Cover the surface of the beet jelly with plastic wrap. Let cool completely.

4. In a stand mixer fitted with a whisk attachment, whisk the mascarpone cheese until smooth. Gradually add the beet jelly and whisk until the mixture is smooth and homogenous [11].

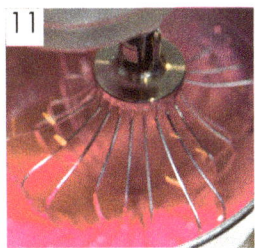
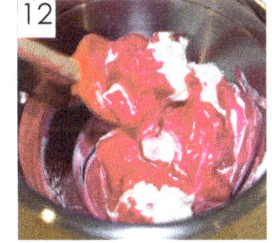

5. Whisk the chilled heavy cream to stiff peaks using a mixer or by hand. Gently fold the whipped cream into the beet-mascarpone cheese mixture until well combined [12]. Chill the cream in the refrigerator for about 2 hours until the cream is set.

Assembly and Decoration:

1. Use a 1-cm/0.38-in fine star tip (#864) to punch a hole in the bottom of each chou [13].

2. Fill a large pastry bag (45.7-cm/18-in) fitted with a 0.8-cm/0.31-in plain tip (#803) with the beet balsamic cream. Pipe the cream into each chou through the hole in the bottom [14].

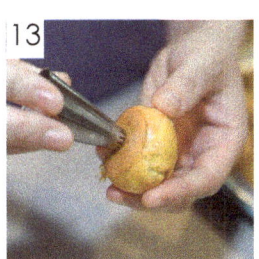
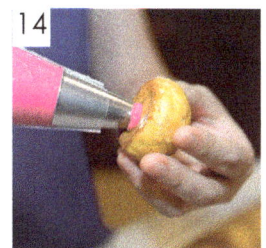

VEGGIES

CARROTS

The addition of fresh carrot juice in the choux paste adds flavor and color whereas chopped cashew nuts elevate the texture of the final product. The carrot mousseline cream is rich but offers a healthy note. This is truly a dessert that tastes good and is good for you as well.

Yield: about 50 3.8-cm/1.5-in mini choux

INGREDIENTS

Carrot Choux:

120 g/4.2 oz all-purpose flour

100 g/3.5 oz whole milk

100 g/3.5 oz fresh carrot juice

2 g/0.071 oz (¼ tsp) kosher salt or fine sea salt

5 g/0.18 oz (1 tsp) granulated sugar

80 g/2.8 oz unsalted butter

200 g/7.1 oz whole eggs (about 4 eggs)

1 whole egg for egg wash

80 g/2.8 oz chopped cashew nuts

Pearl sugar

Carrot Mousseline Cream:

60 g/2.1 oz egg yolks

40 g/1.4 oz granulated sugar (A)

23 g/0.81 oz cornstarch

200 g/7.1 oz whole milk

100 g/3.5 oz fresh carrot juice

20 g/0.71 oz granulated sugar (B)

Carrot Choux:

1. Sift the flour onto a piece of parchment paper. Transfer the sifted flour to a bowl and reserve.

2. Combine the milk, carrot juice, salt, sugar, and butter in a large stainless steel saucepan; heat the mixture over medium-high heat [1].

3. When the mixture comes to a boil, remove the saucepan from heat. Carefully whisk the sifted flour into the mixture [2, 3]. When all the flour is incorporated into the liquid, shake off lumps of dough from the whisk and switch to a spatula or wooden spoon.

4. Return the saucepan to medium-low heat. Stir the paste using a folding motion to remove any remaining small lumps of flour. Continue to cook for 2 to 3 minutes; stir constantly, using a folding motion to bring the dough pieces together, until a smooth and thick paste is obtained.

5. Transfer the dough to a mixer bowl. Attach the bowl to a mixer fitted with a paddle attachment. Mix the dough at medium speed for 10 to 15 seconds to release the steam.

6. Add the eggs one at a time while continuing to mix on medium speed. Make sure each egg is incorporated before adding additional eggs. Scrape down the sides of the mixer bowl with a spatula if necessary. Increase the mixer speed to high. Mix for 10 to 20 seconds or until a smooth paste forms.

7. Meanwhile, line a half-sheet baking pan with a silicone baking mat or parchment paper. Preheat the oven to 191°C/375°F.

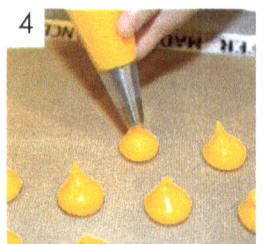

15 g/0.53 oz (1 Tbsp) maple syrup

3 g/0.11 oz (1 tsp) finely grated fresh ginger

20 g/0.71 oz unsalted butter (A), at room temperature

150 g/5.3 oz unsalted butter (B), at room temperature

8. Fill a large pastry bag (45.7-cm/18-in) fitted with a 1.3-cm/0.5-in plain tip (#806) with the choux paste. Pipe the paste into 2.5-cm/1-in mounds with 2.5-cm/1-in spacing on the baking mat or parchment paper [4]. Brush the top with egg wash using a gentle dabbing motion. Sprinkle chopped cashew nuts and pearl sugar on top [5].

9. Bake at 191°C/375°F for about 13 minutes until the choux are puffed up. Reduce the temperature to 177°C/350°F and bake for another 12 minutes until the choux are golden brown. Turn off the oven and leave the choux in the oven undisturbed for another 6 minutes. Remove the baked choux from the oven and let cool completely [6].

Carrot Mousseline Cream:

1. Combine egg yolks, sugar (A), and cornstarch in a stainless steel mixing bowl. Mix well with a balloon whisk. Set aside.

2. Place the milk, carrot juice, sugar (B), maple syrup, and grated ginger in a medium-sized stainless steel saucepan. Heat the milk mixture over medium-high heat. Remove from heat when it comes to a boil.

3. Pour about half of the hot liquid into the reserved egg yolk mixture while whisking vigorously [7]. Pour the mixture back into the pan. Cook the mixture over medium-low heat while whisking constantly for 1 to 2 minutes until the mixture thickens [8]. Let cool slightly. Stir in the softened butter (A) and mix well. Cover the surface of the carrot pastry cream with plastic wrap. Let cool to room temperature.

4. Place the carrot pastry cream in a mixer bowl. Beat with a stand mixer fitted with a wire whisk attachment on medium-high speed until the cream is smooth. Reduce the mixer speed to medium-low and whisk in the softened butter (B) in small increments. Make sure each addition of butter is thoroughly incorporated before adding more. Scrape down the sides of the bowl with a spatula if necessary.

5. Once all the butter is incorporated, adjust the mixer speed to medium-high. Continue to beat for a few more minutes until the cream is light and fluffy [9]. Reserve.

Assembly and Decoration:

1. Use a 1-cm/0.38-in fine star tip (#864) to punch a hole in the bottom of each chou.

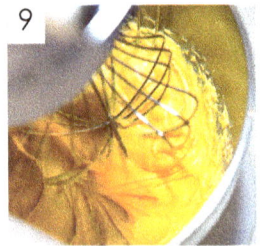
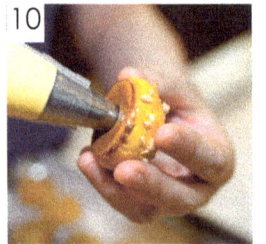

2. Fill a large pastry bag (45.7-cm/18-in) fitted with a 0.8-cm/0.31-in plain tip (#803) with the carrot mousseline cream. Pipe the cream into each chou through the hole in the bottom [10].

ZUCCHINI DOUGHNUTS

This savory-to-sweet transformation offers a refreshing twist on the familiar fritter. These are light, airy, and crispy. The addition of fresh zucchini adds texture and complexity to this simple yet thought-provoking dessert.

Yield: about 30 5-cm/2-in round doughnuts

Ingredients

120 g/4.2 oz all-purpose flour

180 g/6.3 oz fresh zucchini juice

2 g/0.071 oz (¼ tsp) kosher salt or fine sea salt

2 g/0.071 oz (¼ tsp) ground black pepper

5 g/0.18 oz (1 tsp) granulated sugar

80 g/2.8 oz extra-virgin olive oil

200 g/7.1 oz whole eggs (about 4 eggs)

50 g/1.8 oz parmesan cheese, finely grated

100 g/3.5 oz shredded zucchini, with excess juice removed

Peanut oil for frying

Powdered sugar or doughnut sugar for dusting

1. Sift the flour onto a piece of parchment paper. Transfer the sifted flour to a bowl and reserve.

2. Combine the zucchini juice, salt, pepper, sugar, and olive oil in a large stainless steel saucepan; heat the mixture over medium-high heat [1].

3. When the mixture comes to a boil, remove the saucepan from heat. Carefully whisk the sifted flour into the mixture [2]. When all the flour is incorporated into the liquid, shake off lumps of dough from the whisk and switch to a spatula or wooden spoon.

4. Return the saucepan to medium-low heat. Stir the paste using a folding motion to remove any remaining small lumps of flour. Continue to cook for 2 to 3 minutes; stir constantly, using a folding motion to bring the dough pieces together, until a smooth and thick paste is obtained [3].

5. Transfer the dough to a mixer bowl. Attach the bowl to a mixer fitted with a paddle attachment. Mix the dough at medium speed for 10 to 15 seconds to release the steam [4].

6. Add the eggs one at a time while continuing to mix on medium speed [5]. Make sure each egg is incorporated before adding additional eggs. Scrape down the sides of the mixer bowl with a spatula if necessary. Increase the mixer speed to high. Mix for 10 to 20 seconds or until a smooth paste forms [6].

7. Fold the grated parmesan cheese and shredded zucchini into the paste [7–9]. Cover the surface of the choux paste with plastic wrap. Chill the paste in the refrigerator for about an hour.

8. Heat the oil in a Dutch oven or deep fryer to 185°C/365°F.

9. Remove the chilled zucchini choux paste from the refrigerator. Use a 3.8-cm/1.5-in ice cream scoop, preferably with a spring action release, to scoop up the choux paste and carefully drop it into the hot oil [10].

10. Fry the doughnuts for 7 to 9 minutes until they are golden brown and puffed up [11]. Turn the doughnuts over half way during cooking.

11. Remove the doughnuts from the hot oil. Drain excess oil on paper towels. Coat the doughnuts with powdered sugar or doughnut sugar [12]. Serve immediately.

RED PEPPER AND MANGO

This is the ultimate sweet-savory indulgence. The red pepper and olive oil provide the savory note while the mango and cream cheese bring out the sweeter side of this creation. Served in cocktail glasses, it can be enjoyed as an appetizer or dessert. I use a juicer to extract the red pepper juice, but if a juicer is not available, you can use a food processor to puree the peppers and then strain the juice from the puree.

Yield: about 15 individual servings

INGREDIENTS

Red Pepper Chou-Dots and Chou-Sticks:

90 g/3.2 oz all-purpose flour

30 g/1.1 oz semolina pasta flour

130 g/4.6 oz distilled water

50 g/1.8 oz fresh sweet red bell pepper juice

2 g/0.071 oz (¼ tsp) kosher salt or fine sea salt

5 g/0.18 oz (1 tsp) granulated sugar

80 g/2.8 oz extra-virgin olive oil

200 g/7.1 oz whole eggs (about 4 eggs)

Ground pink peppercorns

Turbinado sugar

Red Bell Pepper Cream:

5 g/0.18 oz gelatin sheet (silver grade) or 4.2 g/0.15 oz powdered gelatin + 25.2 g/0.89 oz cold water

150 g/5.3 oz fresh sweet red bell pepper juice

40 g/1.4 oz granulated sugar

150 g/5.3 oz cream cheese, at room temperature

Red Pepper Chou-Dots and Chou-Sticks:

1. Sift the flours onto a piece of parchment paper. Transfer the sifted flours to a bowl and reserve.

2. Combine the water, red pepper juice, salt, sugar, and olive oil in a large stainless steel saucepan; heat the mixture over medium-high heat [1].

3. When the mixture comes to a boil, remove the saucepan from heat. Carefully whisk the sifted flour into the mixture [2]. When all the flour is incorporated into the liquid, shake off lumps of dough from the whisk and switch to a spatula or wooden spoon.

4. Return the saucepan to medium-low heat. Stir the paste using a folding motion to remove any remaining small lumps of flour [3]. Continue to cook for 2 to 3 minutes; stir constantly, using a folding motion to bring the dough pieces together, until a smooth and thick paste is obtained.

5. Transfer the dough to a mixer bowl. Attach the bowl to a mixer fitted with a paddle attachment. Mix the dough at medium speed for 10 to 15 seconds to release the steam.

6. Add the eggs one at a time while continuing to mix on medium speed [4]. Make sure each egg is incorporated before adding additional eggs. Scrape down the sides of the mixer bowl with a spatula if necessary. Increase the mixer speed to high. Mix for 10 to 20 seconds or until a smooth paste forms.

7. Meanwhile, line a half-sheet baking pan with a silicone baking mat or parchment paper. Preheat the oven to 191°C/375°F.

200 g/7.1 oz heavy whipping cream

Mango and Ginger Cream:

2.5 g/0.088 oz gelatin sheet (silver grade) or 2.1 g/0.074 oz powdered gelatin + 12.6 g/0.44 oz cold water

220 g/7.8 oz mango puree

30 g/1.1 oz granulated sugar

3 g/0.11 oz (1 tsp) finely grated fresh ginger

15 g/0.53 oz cornstarch

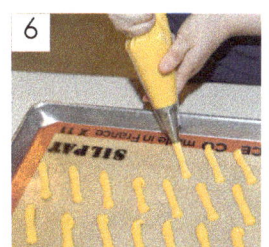

8. Fill a large pastry bag (45.7-cm/18-in) fitted with a 1-cm/0.38-in plain tip (#804) with the choux paste. Pipe the paste into 0.64-cm/0.25-in dots or 3.8-cm/1.5-in sticks on the baking mat or parchment paper [5, 6]. Sprinkle ground pink peppercorns and Turbinado sugar on top.

9. Bake at 191°C/375°F for about 10 minutes for chou-dots or 13 minutes for chou-sticks. Reduce the temperature to 177°C/350°F and bake for another 5 minutes until the choux are golden brown. Turn off the oven and leave the choux in the oven undisturbed for another 5 minutes. Remove the baked choux from the oven and let cool completely [7, 8].

Red Bell Pepper Cream:

1. In a medium-sized bowl, bloom the sheet gelatin in plenty of cold water. If powdered gelatin is used, sprinkle the powder over 25.2 g/0.89 oz cold water in the bowl. Let the gelatin bloom for at least 10 minutes before using.

2. Combine the fresh red pepper juice and sugar in a medium-sized stainless steel saucepan. Mix well with a balloon whisk [9]. Bring the mixture to 71°C/160°F over medium-high heat. Let cool slightly.

3. Meanwhile, squeeze excess water out of the bloomed sheet gelatin and add the gelatin to the pepper mixture [10]. If powdered gelatin is used, add the entire contents to the pepper mixture. Stir to combine. Cover the surface of the pepper jelly with plastic wrap. Let cool completely.

4. In a stand mixer fitted with a whisk attachment, whisk the cream cheese until smooth. Gradually add the pepper jelly and whisk until the mixture is smooth and homogenous [11].

5. Whisk the chilled heavy cream to stiff peaks using a mixer or by hand. Gently fold the whipped cream into the pepper-cream cheese mixture until well combined [12]. Chill the cream in the refrigerator for about 2 hours until the cream is set.

Mango and Ginger Cream:

1. In a medium-sized bowl, bloom the sheet gelatin in plenty of cold water. If powdered gelatin is used, sprinkle the powder over 12.6 g/0.44 oz cold water in the bowl. Let the gelatin bloom for at least 10 minutes before using.

2. Combine the mango puree, sugar, grated ginger, and cornstarch in a medium-sized stainless steel saucepan. Mix well with a balloon whisk. Bring the mixture to a boil over medium-high heat while whisking constantly [13]. Remove from heat when the mixture thickens. Let cool slightly.

3. Meanwhile, squeeze excess water out of the bloomed sheet gelatin and add the gelatin to the mango mixture [14]. If powdered gelatin is used, add the entire con-

 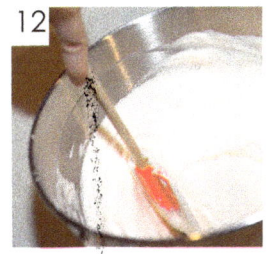

tents to the mango mixture. Stir to combine. Cover the surface of the mango cream with plastic wrap. Let cool completely.

Assembly and Decoration:

1. Fill a large pastry bag (45.7-cm/18-in) fitted with a 1-cm/0.38-in star tip (#824) with the red bell pepper cream. Pipe some pepper cream into a small dessert or cocktail glass [15].

2. Fill another large pastry bag (45.7-cm/18-in) fitted with a 0.64-cm/0.25-in plain tip (#802) with the mango and ginger cream. Pipe some mango and ginger cream on top of the pepper cream [16].

3. Arrange the chou-dots or chou-sticks in the glass [17]. Add more layers of cream and choux [18, 19]. Serve with a dessert spoon.

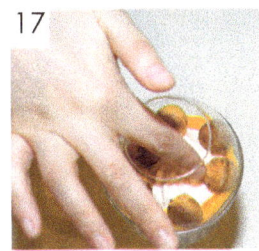 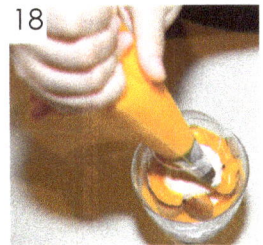

5. CLASSIC

CREAM PUFFS

Simple yet elegant. The classic cream puff will never go out of style. I prefer to use mascarpone cheese in addition to the fresh cream in the Chantilly cream filling since mascarpone cheese adds richness and texture. However, you can replace the cheese with fresh cream. The flavoring of the cream is also optional. In this recipe, I use orange liqueur, but other flavors such as vanilla, almond, coffee, or cherry can also produce excellent results.

Yield: about 32 5-cm/2-in cream puffs

INGREDIENTS

Cream Puff Choux:

120 g/4.2 oz all-purpose flour

100 g/3.5 oz distilled water

100 g/3.5 oz whole milk

2 g/0.071 oz (¼ tsp) kosher salt or fine sea salt

5 g/0.18 oz (1 tsp) granulated sugar

80 g/2.8 oz unsalted butter

200 g/7.1 oz whole eggs (about 4 eggs)

1 whole egg for egg wash

Mascarpone Chantilly Cream:

100 g/3.5 oz mascarpone cheese

300 g/10.6 oz heavy whipping cream

50 g/1.8 oz granulated sugar

15 g/0.53 oz (1 Tbsp) orange liqueur (optional)

Assembly and Decoration:

Powdered sugar for dusting

Cream Puff Choux:

1. Sift the flour onto a piece of parchment paper. Transfer the sifted flour to a bowl and reserve.

2. Combine the water, milk, salt, sugar, and butter in a large stainless steel saucepan; heat the mixture over medium-high heat [1].

3. When the mixture comes to a boil, remove the saucepan from heat. Carefully whisk the sifted flour into the mixture [2, 3]. When all the flour is incorporated into the liquid, shake off lumps of dough from the whisk and switch to a spatula or wooden spoon.

4. Return the saucepan to medium-low heat. Stir the paste using a folding motion to remove any remaining small lumps of flour. Continue to cook for 2 to 3 minutes; stir constantly, using a folding motion to bring the dough pieces together, until a smooth and thick paste is obtained [4].

5. Transfer the dough to a mixer bowl. Attach the bowl to a mixer fitted with a paddle attachment. Mix the dough at medium speed for 10 to 15 seconds to release the steam [5].

6. Add the eggs one at a time while continuing to mix on medium speed [6]. Make sure each egg is incorporated before adding additional eggs. Scrape down the sides of the mixer bowl with a spatula if necessary. Increase the mixer speed to high. Mix for 10 to 20 seconds or until a smooth paste forms [7].

7. Meanwhile, line a half-sheet baking pan with a silicone baking mat or parchment paper. Preheat the oven to 191°C/375°F.

8. Fill a large pastry bag (45.7-cm/18-in) fitted with a 1.6-cm/0.63-in plain tip (#808) with the choux paste. Pipe the paste into 3.2-cm/1.25-in mounds with 2.5-cm/1-in spacing on the baking mat or parchment paper [8]. Brush the top with egg wash using a gentle dabbing motion [9].

9. Bake at 191°C/375°F for about 15 minutes until the choux are puffed up. Reduce the temperature to 177°C/350°F and bake for another 13 minutes until the choux are golden brown. Turn off the oven and leave the choux in the oven undisturbed for another 10 minutes. Remove the baked choux from the oven and let cool completely.

Mascarpone Chantilly Cream:

1. In a mixer bowl, combine the mascarpone cheese, heavy cream, sugar, and liqueur.

2. Attach the mixer bowl to a mixer fitted with a whisk attachment. Whisk the mixture on medium speed until the mixture thickens slightly. Increase the speed to high and whisk the mixture until stiff peaks form [10]. Do not over-beat.

Assembly and Decoration:

1. Using a serrated knife, cut off the top ⅓ of each chou and reserve the cap [11].

2. Fill a large pastry bag (45.7-cm/18-in) fitted with a 0.8-cm/0.31-in closed star tip (#843) with the mascarpone Chantilly cream.

3. Pipe the cream into the bottom portion of the chou [12]. Place the reserved cap on top of the cream [13]. Dust the top with powdered sugar if desired [14].

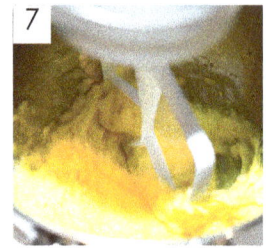

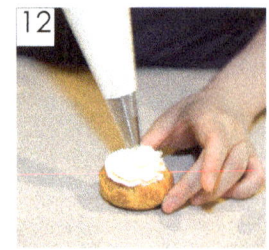

CARAMEL

Sea salt-caramel is another crowd-pleasing classic. The crunchy peanut topping is the perfect companion for the sweet, nutty, creamy caramel filling.

Yield: about 32 5-cm/2-in choux

INGREDIENTS

Round Choux with Peanut Topping:

120 g/4.2 oz all-purpose flour

100 g/3.5 oz distilled water

100 g/3.5 oz whole milk

2 g/0.071 oz (¼ tsp) kosher salt or fine sea salt

5 g/0.18 oz (1 tsp) granulated sugar

80 g/2.8 oz unsalted butter

200 g/7.1 oz whole eggs (about 4 eggs)

1 whole egg for egg wash

80 g/2.8 oz chopped peanuts (optional)

Caramel Cream:

150 g/5.3 oz heavy whipping cream (A)

150 g/5.3 oz granulated sugar

Pinch of sea salt

150 g/5.3 oz mascarpone cheese, at room temperature

200 g/7.1 oz heavy whipping cream (B)

Round Choux with Peanut Topping:

1. Sift the flour onto a piece of parchment paper. Transfer the sifted flour to a bowl and reserve.

2. Combine the water, milk, salt, sugar, and butter in a large stainless steel saucepan; heat the mixture over medium-high heat.

3. When the mixture comes to a boil, remove the saucepan from heat. Carefully whisk the sifted flour into the mixture. When all the flour is incorporated into the liquid, shake off lumps of dough from the whisk and switch to a spatula or wooden spoon.

4. Return the saucepan to medium-low heat. Stir the paste using a folding motion to remove any remaining small lumps of flour. Continue to cook for 2 to 3 minutes; stir constantly, using a folding motion to bring the dough pieces together, until a smooth and thick paste is obtained.

5. Transfer the dough to a mixer bowl. Attach the bowl to a mixer fitted with a paddle attachment. Mix the dough at medium speed for 10 to 15 seconds to release the steam.

6. Add the eggs one at a time while continuing to mix on medium speed. Make sure each egg is incorporated before adding additional eggs. Scrape down the sides of the mixer bowl with a spatula if necessary. Increase the mixer speed to high. Mix for 10 to 20 seconds or until a smooth paste forms [1].

7. Meanwhile, line a half-sheet baking pan with a silicone baking mat or parchment paper. Preheat the oven to 191°C/375°F.

8. Fill a large pastry bag (45.7-cm/18-in) fitted with a 1.6-cm/0.63-in plain tip (#808) with the choux paste.

Pipe the paste into 3.2-cm/1.25-in mounds with 2.5-cm/1-in spacing on the baking mat or parchment paper [2]. Brush the top with egg wash using a gentle dabbing motion [3]. Sprinkle the choux with chopped peanuts if desired [4].

9. Bake at 191°C/375°F for about 15 minutes until the choux are puffed up. Reduce the temperature to 177°C/350°F and bake for another 13 minutes until the choux are golden brown. Turn off the oven and leave the choux in the oven undisturbed for another 10 minutes. Remove the baked choux from the oven and let cool completely [5].

Caramel Cream:

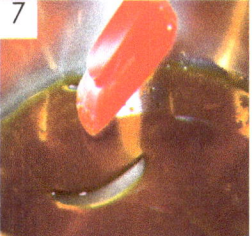

1. To make the caramel, place the heavy cream (A) in a medium-sized stainless steel saucepan and set aside.

2. Place the sugar in a large stainless steel saucepan in an even layer. Dry melt the sugar over medium heat undisturbed for 3 to 5 minutes.

3. Meanwhile, heat the cream over high heat. Remove the pan from heat when the cream comes to a boil. Reserve.

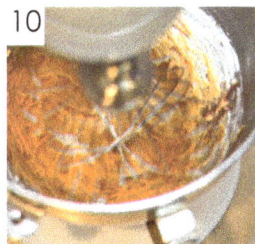

4. When most of the sugar underneath the top layer of granules is melted and has turned a golden color, reduce the heat to low. Stir occasionally with a spatula to avoid burning the caramel [6].

5. When all of the sugar is melted and the caramel turns medium-dark amber at around 180°C/356°F [7], pour the hot cream into the pan [8]. Stir vigorously to smooth out any lumps. Continue to cook the caramel for another 2 to 3 minutes while stirring constantly [9]. Cook until the caramel is smooth and velvety. Remove from heat, add salt, and stir to combine.

6. Let the caramel cool slightly. Cover the surface of the caramel directly with plastic wrap. Allow the caramel to cool completely before using it.

7. In a stand mixer fitted with a whisk attachment, whisk the mascarpone cheese and caramel until smooth [10]. Whisk the chilled heavy cream (B) to medium peaks using a mixer or by hand. Gently fold the whipped cream into the caramel-mascarpone cheese mixture until well combined [11]. Reserve the cream in the refrigerator until ready to use.

Assembly and Decoration:

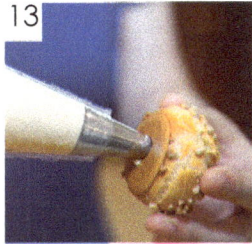

1. Use a 1-cm/0.38-in fine star tip (#864) to punch a hole in the bottom of each chou [12].

2. Fill a large pastry bag (45.7-cm/18-in) fitted with a 0.8-cm/0.31-in plain tip (#803) with the caramel cream. Pipe the cream into each chou through the hole in the bottom [13].

CHOCOLATE

Who can resist the rich, decadent chocolate éclair? Now they are in miniature form, but with the same tantalizing taste. Be sure to use high-quality chocolate couverture in this recipe to optimize the result. The chocolate glaze should be made a day in advance so that it can set properly.

Yield: about 30 6.4-cm/2.5-in mini éclairs

INGREDIENTS

Chocolate Glaze:

10 g/0.35 oz sheet gelatin (silver grade) or 8.3 g/0.29 oz powdered gelatin + 50 g/1.8 oz cold water

90 g/3.2 oz unsweetened, Dutch-processed cocoa powder

175 g/6.2 oz heavy whipping cream

250 g/8.8 oz granulated sugar

90 g/3.2 oz distilled water

Mini Éclairs:

120 g/4.2 oz all-purpose flour

100 g/3.5 oz distilled water

100 g/3.5 oz whole milk

2 g/0.071 oz (¼ tsp) kosher salt or fine sea salt

5 g/0.18 oz (1 tsp) granulated sugar

80 g/2.8 oz unsalted butter

200 g/7.1 oz whole eggs (about 4 eggs)

1 whole egg for egg wash

Chocolate Glaze:

1. In a medium-sized bowl, bloom the sheet gelatin in plenty of cold water. If using powdered gelatin, sprinkle the powder over 50 g/1.8 oz cold water in the bowl. Let the gelatin bloom for at least 10 minutes before using.

2. Meanwhile, sift the cocoa powder and set aside.

3. Combine the cream, sugar, and water in a large stainless-steel saucepan. Bring the mixture to a boil over medium-high heat.

4. Reduce the heat to low and whisk in the sifted cocoa powder [1]. Whisk constantly and cook the mixture for 1 to 2 minutes [2]. Remove from heat and let cool slightly.

5. Meanwhile, squeeze excess water out of the bloomed sheet gelatin and add the gelatin to the mixture [3]. If using powdered gelatin, add the entire contents to the mixture. Whisk to combine.

6. Transfer the chocolate glaze mixture to a medium-sized mixing bowl. Use an immersion blender to blend the mixture until it is smooth and glossy [4].

7. Cover the surface of the chocolate glaze with plastic wrap. Chill in the refrigerator overnight before using.

Mini Éclairs:

1. Sift the flour onto a piece of parchment paper. Transfer the sifted flour to a bowl and reserve.

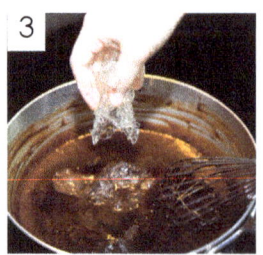

Chocolate Diploma Cream:

45 g/1.6 oz egg yolks

25 g/0.88 oz granulated sugar (A)

15 g/0.53 oz cornstarch

230 g/8.1 oz whole milk

25 g/0.88 oz granulated sugar (B)

90 g/3.2 oz bittersweet dark chocolate couverture, finely chopped

45 g/1.6 oz unsalted butter, at room temperature

210 g/7.4 oz heavy whipping cream

2. Combine the water, milk, salt, sugar, and butter in a large stainless steel saucepan; heat the mixture over medium-high heat.

3. When the mixture comes to a boil, remove the saucepan from heat. Carefully whisk the sifted flour into the mixture. When all the flour is incorporated into the liquid, shake off lumps of dough from the whisk and switch to a spatula or wooden spoon.

4. Return the saucepan to medium-low heat. Stir the paste using a folding motion to remove any remaining small lumps of flour. Continue to cook for 2 to 3 minutes; stir constantly, using a folding motion to bring the dough pieces together, until a smooth and thick paste is obtained.

5. Transfer the dough to a mixer bowl. Attach the bowl to a mixer fitted with a paddle attachment. Mix the dough at medium speed for 10 to 15 seconds to release the steam.

6. Add the eggs one at a time while continuing to mix on medium speed. Make sure each egg is incorporated before adding additional eggs. Scrape down the sides of the mixer bowl with a spatula if necessary. Increase the mixer speed to high. Mix for 10 to 20 seconds or until a smooth paste forms [5].

7. Meanwhile, line a half-sheet baking pan with a silicone baking mat or parchment paper.

8. Preheat the oven to 191°C/375°F. Fill a large pastry bag (45.7-cm/18-in) fitted with a 1.1-cm/0.44-in fine star tip (#865) with the choux paste. Pipe the paste into 6.4-cm/2.5-in logs with 2.5-cm/1-in spacing on the baking mat or parchment paper [6]. Brush the top with egg wash using a gentle dabbing motion [7].

9. Bake at 191°C/375°F for about 15 minutes until the éclairs are puffed up. Reduce the temperature to 177°C/350°F and bake for another 15 minutes until the éclairs are golden brown. Turn off the oven and leave the éclairs in the oven undisturbed for another 10 minutes. Remove the baked éclairs from the oven and let cool completely [8].

Chocolate Diploma Cream:

1. Combine egg yolks, sugar (A), and cornstarch in a stainless steel mixing bowl. Mix well with a balloon whisk [9]. Set aside.

2. Heat the milk and sugar (B) mixture over medium-high heat in a medium-sized stainless steel saucepan. Remove from heat when it comes to a boil. Pour about half of the hot liquid into the reserved egg yolk mixture while whisking vigorously [10]. Pour the mixture back into the pan [11]. Cook the mixture over medium-low heat while whisking constantly for 1 to 2 minutes until the mixture thickens [12]. Remove from heat.

3. Stir in the dark chocolate pieces and mix well [13]. Stir in the softened butter and mix vigorously until the mixture is smooth and homogenous.

4. Cover the surface of the chocolate pastry cream with plastic wrap. Let cool to room temperature.

5. Place the pastry cream in a mixer bowl. Beat with a stand mixer fitted with a wire whisk attachment on medium-high speed until the cream is smooth [14].

6. Whip the chilled heavy cream to stiff peaks by hand or using a mixer. Fold about ⅓ of the whipped cream into the pastry cream using a spatula. Mix until the mixture is homogenous. Gently fold in the remaining ⅔ of the whipped cream [15]. Reserve.

Assembly and Decoration:

1. Use a 1-cm/0.38-in fine star tip (#864) to punch a hole in the bottom of each éclair [16].

2. Fill a large pastry bag (45.7-cm/18-in) fitted with a 0.8-cm/0.31-in plain tip (#803) with the chocolate diploma cream. Pipe the cream into each éclair through the hole in the bottom [17].

3. Gently heat the chocolate glaze in a microwave at 10-second increments and stir the glaze after each heating. Take care not to over-heat the glaze. Use the glaze at 25°C/77°F.

4. Dip the filled éclair into the chocolate glaze [18]. Gently shake off excess glaze and place the éclair bottom-side down on a piece of parchment paper. Repeat until all the éclairs are glazed.

Classic

VANILLA

The perfect companion to chocolate éclairs, these miniature vanilla éclairs are absolutely delightful. You can substitute vanilla extract for the vanilla beans, but I think the use of fresh vanilla beans elevates this dessert significantly. You can use ready-made fondant. However, if you choose to make the fondant, be sure to make it at least a day in advance. You can save the leftover fondant for later uses.

Yield: about 30 6.4-cm/2.5-in mini éclairs

Ingredients

Pastry Fondant (makes about 600 g/21.2 oz fondant):

500 g/17.6 oz granulated sugar

100 g/3.5 oz distilled water

100 g/3.5 oz glucose syrup

Mini Éclairs:

120 g/4.2 oz all-purpose flour

100 g/3.5 oz distilled water

100 g/3.5 oz whole milk

2 g/0.071 oz (¼ tsp) kosher salt or fine sea salt

5 g/0.18 oz (1 tsp) granulated sugar

80 g/2.8 oz unsalted butter

200 g/7.1 oz whole eggs (about 4 eggs)

1 whole egg for egg wash

Vanilla Mousseline Cream:

60 g/2.1 oz egg yolks

40 g/1.4 oz granulated sugar (A)

Pastry Fondant (makes about 600 g/21.2 oz fondant):

1. Combine the sugar and water in a medium-sized stainless steel saucepan. Heat the mixture over medium heat. Stir constantly with a spatula until the sugar is dissolved.

2. When the sugar syrup comes to a boil, stir in the glucose syrup [1]. Bring the mixture back to a boil.

3. Insert a candy thermometer and stop stirring. Increase the heat to medium-high. Continue to cook the sugar; brush down the sides of the pan with a pastry brush dipped in cold water to prevent sugar crystals from forming.

4. Cook the sugar until it reaches 118°C/244°F. Let cool slightly. Pour the syrup into a food processor [2] and cover the food processor bowl tightly with plastic wrap.

5. Let the syrup cool to 80°C/176°F. Turn on the food processor. Mix until the syrup turns opaque, white, and glossy [3].

6. Immediately transfer the white fondant into a plastic bag or other container. Cover and let it rest at room temperature overnight before using it. The fondant will become softer and more pliable.

Mini Éclairs:

1. Sift the flour onto a piece of parchment paper. Transfer the sifted flour to a bowl and reserve.

23 g/0.81 oz cornstarch

300 g/10.6 oz whole milk

35 g/1.2 oz granulated sugar (B)

1 vanilla bean

20 g/0.71 oz unsalted butter (A), at room temperature

150 g/5.3 oz unsalted butter (B), at room temperature

Assembly and Decoration:

45 g/1.6 oz granulated sugar

35 g/1.2 oz distilled water

300 g/10.6 oz pastry fondant

1 vanilla bean

2. Combine the water, milk, salt, sugar, and butter in a large stainless steel saucepan; heat the mixture over medium-high heat.

3. When the mixture comes to a boil, remove the saucepan from heat. Carefully whisk the sifted flour into the mixture [4]. When all the flour is incorporated into the liquid, shake off lumps of dough from the whisk and switch to a spatula or wooden spoon.

4. Return the saucepan to medium-low heat. Stir the paste using a folding motion to remove any remaining small lumps of flour. Continue to cook for 2 to 3 minutes; stir constantly, using a folding motion to bring the dough pieces together, until a smooth and thick paste is obtained.

5. Transfer the dough to a mixer bowl. Attach the bowl to a mixer fitted with a paddle attachment. Mix the dough at medium speed for 10 to 15 seconds to release the steam.

6. Add the eggs one at a time while continuing to mix on medium speed. Make sure each egg is incorporated before adding additional eggs. Scrape down the sides of the mixer bowl with a spatula if necessary. Increase the mixer speed to high. Mix for 10 to 20 seconds or until a smooth paste forms [5].

7. Meanwhile, line a half-sheet baking pan with a silicone baking mat or parchment paper.

8. Preheat the oven to 191°C/375°F. Fill a large pastry bag (45.7-cm/18-in) fitted with a 1.1-cm/0.44-in fine star tip (#865) with the choux paste. Pipe the paste into 6.4-cm/2.5-in logs with 2.5-cm/1-in spacing on the baking mat or parchment paper [6]. Brush the top with egg wash using a gentle dabbing motion [7].

9. Bake at 191°C/375°F for about 15 minutes until the éclairs are puffed up. Reduce the temperature to 177°C/350°F and bake for another 15 minutes until the éclairs are golden brown. Turn off the oven and leave the éclairs in the oven undisturbed for another 10 minutes. Remove the baked éclairs from the oven and let cool completely [8].

Vanilla Mousseline Cream:

1. Combine egg yolks, sugar (A), and cornstarch in a stainless steel mixing bowl. Mix well with a balloon whisk [9]. Set aside.

2. Place the milk and sugar (B) in a medium-sized stainless steel saucepan. Use a paring knife to split the vanilla bean lengthwise. Scrape off the vanilla seeds using the back of the knife [10]. Add the vanilla bean halves and seeds to the saucepan [11].

3. Heat the milk mixture over medium-high heat. Remove from heat when it comes to a boil. Pour about half of the hot liquid into the reserved egg yolk mixture while

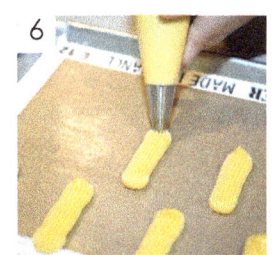

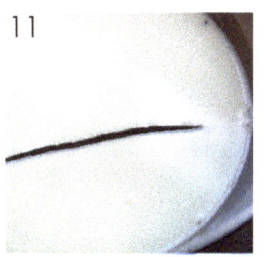

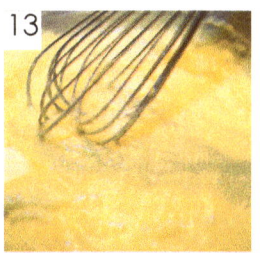
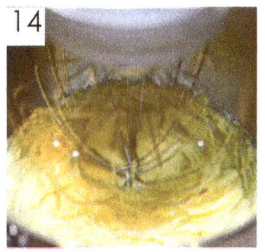

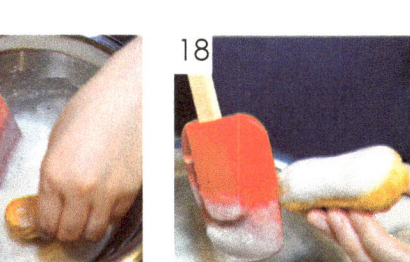

whisking vigorously [12]. Pour the mixture back into the pan. Remove the vanilla bean halves. Cook the mixture over medium-low heat while whisking constantly for 1 to 2 minutes until the mixture thickens. Let cool slightly. Stir in the softened butter (A) and mix well [13].

4. Cover the surface of the pastry cream with plastic wrap. Let cool to room temperature.

5. Place the pastry cream in a mixer bowl. Beat with a stand mixer fitted with a wire whisk attachment on medium-high speed until the cream is smooth.

6. Reduce the mixer speed to medium-low and whisk in the softened butter (B) in small increments. Make sure each addition of butter is thoroughly incorporated before adding more. Scrape down the sides of the bowl with a spatula if necessary.

7. Once all the butter is incorporated, adjust the mixer speed to medium-high. Continue to beat for a few more minutes until the cream is light and fluffy [14]. Reserve.

Assembly and Decoration:

1. Use a 1-cm/0.38-in fine star tip (#864) to punch a hole in the bottom of each éclair [15].

2. Fill a large pastry bag (45.7-cm/18-in) fitted with a 0.8-cm/0.31-in plain tip (#803) with the vanilla mousseline cream. Pipe the cream into each éclair through the hole in the bottom [16].

3. To make the syrup for the vanilla fondant glaze, combine the sugar and water in a medium-sized saucepan. Bring the mixture to a boil and remove from heat. Let the syrup cool slightly.

4. Combine the syrup and pastry fondant in a medium-sized mixing bowl. Use a paring knife to split the vanilla bean lengthwise. Scrape off the vanilla seeds using the back of the knife. Add the vanilla seeds to the mixture.

5. Gently heat the mixture over a double-boiler or in a microwave until the mixture reaches 37°C/98.6°F. Stir to combine. Do not heat the mixture hotter than 50°C/122°F.

6. Dip the filled éclair into the vanilla fondant glaze [17]. Gently shake off excess glaze [18] and place the éclair bottom-side down on a piece of parchment paper. Repeat until all the éclairs are glazed.

Classic

HAZELNUT AND RASPBERRY

The classic combination of hazelnut and raspberry is showcased in this whimsical dessert. Rich hazelnut mousseline cream with a sweet, soft raspberry jam center is embraced by a double-choux and topped with sliced almonds. This dessert will stay in your pastry repertoire.

Yield: about 25 individual pastries

INGREDIENTS

Double Choux with Almond Topping:

120 g/4.2 oz all-purpose flour

100 g/3.5 oz distilled water

100 g/3.5 oz whole milk

2 g/0.071 oz (¼ tsp) kosher salt or fine sea salt

5 g/0.18 oz (1 tsp) granulated sugar

80 g/2.8 oz unsalted butter

200 g/7.1 oz whole eggs (about 4 eggs)

1 whole egg for egg wash

Sliced almonds

Hazelnut Mousseline Cream:

60 g/2.1 oz egg yolks

40 g/1.4 oz granulated sugar (A)

23 g/0.81 oz cornstarch

300 g/10.6 oz whole milk

35 g/1.2 oz granulated sugar (B)

1 vanilla bean

Double Choux with Almond Topping:

1. Sift the flour onto a piece of parchment paper. Transfer the sifted flour to a bowl and reserve.

2. Combine the water, milk, salt, sugar, and butter in a large stainless steel saucepan; heat the mixture over medium-high heat.

3. When the mixture comes to a boil, remove the saucepan from heat. Carefully whisk the sifted flour into the mixture [1]. When all the flour is incorporated into the liquid, shake off lumps of dough from the whisk and switch to a spatula or wooden spoon.

4. Return the saucepan to medium-low heat. Stir the paste using a folding motion to remove any remaining small lumps of flour. Continue to cook for 2 to 3 minutes; stir constantly, using a folding motion to bring the dough pieces together, until a smooth and thick paste is obtained [2].

5. Transfer the dough to a mixer bowl. Attach the bowl to a mixer fitted with a paddle attachment. Mix the dough at medium speed for 10 to 15 seconds to release the steam.

6. Add the eggs one at a time while continuing to mix on medium speed [3]. Make sure each egg is incorporated before adding additional eggs. Scrape down the sides of the mixer bowl with a spatula if necessary. Increase the mixer speed to high. Mix for 10 to 20 seconds or until a smooth paste forms [4].

7. Meanwhile, line a half-sheet baking pan with a silicone baking mat or parchment paper. Preheat the oven to 191°C/375°F.

20 g/0.71 oz unsalted butter (A), at room temperature

150 g/5.3 oz hazelnut praline paste

150 g/5.3 oz unsalted butter (B), at room temperature

Raspberry Jam:

110 g/3.9 oz granulated sugar

6 g/0.21 oz (1½ tsp) powdered pectin NH

150 g/5.3 oz frozen raspberries

150 g/5.3 oz raspberry puree

Assembly and Decoration:

Powdered sugar for dusting

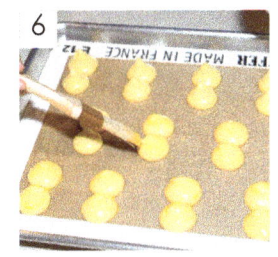

8. Fill a large pastry bag (45.7-cm/18-in) fitted with a 1.3-cm/0.5-in plain tip (#806) with the choux paste. Pipe the paste into 2.5-cm/1-in mound; pipe another mound right below the first mound. Make sure the two mounds are touching [5]. Brush the top with egg wash using a gentle dabbing motion [6]. Sprinkle the choux with sliced almonds if desired [7].

9. Bake at 191°C/375°F for about 17 minutes until the choux are puffed up. Reduce the temperature to 177°C/350°F and bake for another 15 minutes until the choux are golden brown. Turn off the oven and leave the choux in the oven undisturbed for another 10 minutes. Remove the baked choux from the oven and let cool completely [8].

Hazelnut Mousseline Cream:

1. Combine egg yolks, sugar (A), and cornstarch in a stainless steel mixing bowl. Mix well with a balloon whisk [9]. Set aside.

2. Place the milk and sugar (B) in a medium-sized stainless steel saucepan. Use a paring knife to split the vanilla bean lengthwise. Scrape off the vanilla seeds using the back of the knife. Add the vanilla bean halves and seeds to the saucepan.

3. Heat the milk mixture over medium-high heat. Remove from heat when it comes to a boil. Pour about half of the hot liquid into the reserved egg yolk mixture while whisking vigorously [10]. Pour the mixture back into the pan. Remove the vanilla bean halves. Cook the mixture over medium-low heat while whisking constantly for 1 to 2 minutes until the mixture thickens [11]. Let cool slightly. Stir in the softened butter (A) and mix well.

4. Cover the surface of the pastry cream with plastic wrap. Let cool to room temperature.

5. Place the pastry cream and hazelnut praline in a mixer bowl. Beat with a stand mixer fitted with a wire whisk attachment on medium-high speed until the mixture is smooth.

6. Reduce the mixer speed to medium-low and whisk in the softened butter (B) in small increments [12]. Make sure each addition of butter is thoroughly incorporated before adding more. Scrape down the sides of the bowl with a spatula if necessary.

7. Once all the butter is incorporated, adjust the mixer speed to medium-high. Continue to beat for a few more minutes until the cream is light and fluffy. Reserve.

Raspberry Jam:

1. Combine half the sugar and pectin in a mixing bowl. Mix thoroughly and reserve.

2. In a medium-sized stainless steel saucepan, combine the remaining sugar, frozen

raspberries, and raspberry puree [13]. Bring the mixture to a boil over medium-high heat. Stir in the sugar-pectin mixture [14]. Bring the mixture back to a boil and reduce the heat to medium-low. Stir constantly and cook for another 5 minutes [15].

3. Let cool slightly. Cover the surface of the raspberry jam with plastic wrap. Allow the jam to cool completely before using.

Assembly and Decoration:

1. Using a serrated knife, cut off the top ⅓ of each double-choux and reserve the cap [16].

2. Fill a large pastry bag (45.7-cm/18-in) fitted with a 1.3-cm/0.5-in plain tip (#806) with the hazelnut mousseline cream. Pipe two mounds of hazelnut cream into the bottom portion of the choux [17].

3. Fill a medium-sized pastry bag (30.5-cm/12-in) fitted with a 0.6-cm/0.25-in plain tip (#802) with the raspberry jam. Press the tip gently into the hazelnut cream mound and pipe a small amount of the jam in the center [18]. Repeat to fill the second mound.

4. Place the reserved cap on top of the cream [19]. Dust the top with powdered sugar if desired [20].

Classic